We Are the Road Crew

By

Ken Barr

We Are the Road Crew

Life on the Road and How I Got There

By

Ken Barr

Published by:
Dark Alley Publishing
A Division of Dark Alley Studios

Authors note: In this book you will read mostly stories of my days on the road. It's not that I am self centered, rather that I want to respect the privacy of the guys I toured with. If they want to share any stories or pictures, maybe I'll do another book. Let's hope so.

Printed by CreateSpace.com
In the United States of America
Published in 2009 by Dark Alley Publishing
A division of Dark Alley Studios
WWW.DarkAlley-Studios.com
www.myspace.com/darkalleystudios
Inquiries: Kbarr2@cfl.rr.com
2010 Second Edition
Text copyright 2009 by Ken Barr
Photographs copyright 2009 by Ken Barr
Cover concept by Ken Barr
Cover Layout by Roy Louden
Cover copyright 2009 Ken Barr
Cover photo 2000 © Ben Goode
Image from BigStockPhoto.com

Without the love and support of my wife Monica, this book would not be possible. Thank you for always being there.

I would also like to dedicate this work to the memory of my grandparents William and Edith Donnelly. Two people who raised their children, grandchildren, great grandchildren, and many other people's children. They raised me and I miss them every day.

As all things start with family, I would like to thank mine for their contributions to my life.

Thank you to all those that gave me the opportunities I had on the road, and to all my road brothers out there.

Emma and Darla, you are always in my heart.

The Barr girls; Lucy, Pebs and Abbey, you bring light and love into my life every day.

Thank you ......

The Alice Cooper Organization; Alice, Shep, Toby, and Brian

The KISS Organization

The Gibson Family

Mr. Udo and all at Udo Artists

Eric Singer, Derek Sherinian, John Miceli, John Roggio, Tommy Henriksen, Johnny Caswell, Greg Smith, Louie Appel, George Cintron, Joe Lynn Turner, George Silk, Karl Cochran, Gary Corbett, Angus Vail, Andre Augustine, Al Fritsch, Todd Jensen, Ryan Roxie, Teri Hatcher, Russell Dannecker, The Botting Family, Bruce Kulick, Todd's parents- Mr. and Mrs. Confessore, Ralph's parents- Mr. and Mrs. Ferreri, Vinnie's family-The Kowalskis, Johns parents – Mr. and Mrs. Miceli, Al's parents – Mr. and Mrs. Pitrelli, The Seymour Family, Paul Duffy and all at The Irish Rover in Sarasota, Fl., John Karlquist, Fiddlers Green in Winter Park, Fl., Rob "Super Roadie" Belcher, Kevin "Batty" Walsh, Putter T, Dan Stevenson, Scott Hennessy, Charlie Hernandez, Jeff Mann, Kevin "Tater" McCarthy, Trapps the Boy Wonder, The Almighty, Stone Temple Pilots, John O'Reilly, Al Pitrelli, Jimmy DeGrasso, The Bangles, Air Supply, Ritchie Mazzetta, Kenny Sherry, Ritchie Blackmore, Blake Elkin, Jimmy Gregorek, Raymie Kopels, Todd Confessore, Vinnie Kowalski, Ralph Ferreri, Charlie Milton, Howie Thaler, Carl Davino, and all the bands on Long Island that gave me a gig over the years.

We are the Road Crew

Somewhere, sometime if you have ever been to a concert, whether you realized it or not there was an army of technicians there putting the show together and keeping it running. If they were doing their job, you didn't know they were there, but they were. The road crew. Most people don't even realize there is a crew, they are there from the early morning setting up, through the show, and late into the night tearing the show down and putting it back into the trucks so they can get to tomorrows show.

Any show out there is going to have its own army of riggers, carpenters, sound and light crews, video crew, security team, pyro crew, laser people, production and stage managers, and the band gear or backline crew. All these people work together with the local stagehand crew do an amazing amount of work in a relatively short time.

I spent the better part of my adult life on the road and I loved every day of it. Nowadays they have schools where kids can learn the basic skills needed to get a job on the road. But when I started out these schools either didn't exist, or if they did I didn't know about them. Back then we all started out working local bar gigs, where you learned a little of everything and everyone did it all. That's where my story starts, the local bars of Long Island, New York.

The First Gig

Having learned the very basics in high school, which end of the microphone to yell into among other things, I realized I knew all there was to know about putting on a show, how hard could it be? Like most crew guys I started out as a rock star wannabe. I played guitar and started a band, I was on my way. The town I grew up in was small and there really weren't any clubs as such to play in. As kids we convinced the owners of the local taverns, gin mills for the working man, to let us set up in the corner and play. We were allowed to charge a small cover which the bar owner would then give us a percentage of, or so we thought.

There were only a couple of bands in the school I went to, and as I said very few places to play. When one band would get a gig at the local bar, the rest of us would become the crew, carrying in equipment in milk crates in hopes of avoiding the cover charge, and possibly getting to mooch from the bands bar tab. The phrase "I'm with the band" has gotten me many a free drink over the years.

The first gig that I actually recall was a neighborhood bar called "Schultzes Tuck Inn" , it was a massive building with a four sided bar right by the front door, and a couple of pool tables further back. Behind that was just a large darkness, the place was poorly lit and there was no reason to go beyond the pool tables. I spent many a Saturday afternoon as a kid in Schultzes, sipping cokes and playing shuffleboard as my parents drank with their friends. Eventually someone ventured into the darkness at the back of the building and realized there was a full-size stage there.

Nobody seemed to realize it was there, and the owner couldn't seem to remember why it was there or if it had ever been used.

The gig at Schultzes was an enormous event that took weeks of planning, an army of friends to help, hand made flyers, a PA "borrowed" from school. This was bigger than Woodstock. The lights we had were made from tomato sauce cans that our friend from the pizza place saved for us, the really large ones. The bulbs, I am sorry to say, were borrowed from a local airport runway. This was back when you could drive right to a runway, not like today. It never occurred to us that taking the runway lights might be bad. We were kind of like the little rascals that way; everything seemed like a good idea.

The gig itself almost seems uneventful after the weeks of planning. Songs were played, people danced, bar tabs were rung up. But it was the planning, the putting together of this massive event that stands out in my memory.

This gig led to others, a lot of bars where we kids weren't really welcome. We didn't care. When you are under the legal drinking age but either in or with the band, nobody thinks to proof you. It is assumed you are legal. Not only that, on the nights when you aren't playing you could go to a bar where you were known and drink, and often times the bartender wouldn't charge you because you were a regular. This may not seem like much now, but to a kid of 15 or 16 back in the seventies, this was heaven.

Ken Barr circa 1979

The Steady Night

Key in the business when you are starting out is getting a "steady night" somewhere. This is when you play the same place the same day of the week, every week. This is important for building a following, if you are good, or just having steady employment and a place to practice if you aren't so good. The typical way this is done is to talk a bar owner into giving you a shot, usually on a night the bar wouldn't be crowded anyway, like a Sunday.

Once you get your shot, normally for a piece of what comes in the door, you get everyone you know to show up. Beg and plead if you have to. Promise favors, whatever it takes. On the big night when the bar is more packed than it's ever been, the owner will be in a good mood to negotiate a fair price for a steady night.

It was this way that I got my first steady night. It was at a little side of the road dump of a bar called "The Purple Onion". The band managed to procure Sunday nights for the summer, and I was the crew. On our first night the place was so mobbed you couldn't move. I don't know if the place had a fire code restriction, but if it did we were way past it.

At the end of the night we struck the deal. We would be paid $200 a night for every Sunday all summer. Five sets a night, starting at 9 o'clock. We were stoked, a steady night. New songs were learned, clothes were bought. We got to the Onion early to set up and get ready. About 7 you could tell things were not going to go as planned. Nobody came. We waited and waited, but nobody came. We held the first set for a while, but still no one.

It turned out that everyone we knew had come the first night and that was enough. Whether the band wasn't that good, or the fact that most had summer jobs and they had to get up, I will never know. Either way, we were skunked. The owner was cool and paid us for the night, but also renegotiated. He definitely saw the writing on the wall. We would continue to get paid, but it would be a door deal. The more people that came, the more we made. If no one came, no money. Fair enough.

The following Sunday we arrived at the Onion at our usual time and the bartender, Orst, let us in. We set up as usual and got ready. And we got skunked again. This meant that not only were we not getting paid, but our new bartender friend wasn't going to make any money either.

About 10 p.m. Orst threw in the towel and declared the night a bust. With that, he pulled out a blender and started making something he called a "piña colada". As I had only had beers and some shots here and there until that point, this was foreign territory to me. I don't remember much about that summer, but I will always remember Orst for introducing me to the Frozen Drink that night.

Sundays that summer continued to be a bust. They turned into a free hangout and free booze for us and Orst. It didn't take the owner all that long to realize we were drinking him out of business, so by August he figured he would just stay closed on Sundays. We had lost our first home.

The Mailing List

Before the days of the internet, the best way for a band to self promote was to have a mailing list. This was a list compiled by walking around the bar in between sets with a notebook, and asking people to be on your mailing list. They would write down their address, and every month we would send out a pre-printed postcard with where we would be for the entire month. The reason this is important is because if you are playing at "The Dublin Pub" it is not cool to tell people you are playing "The Quarterdeck Saloon" tomorrow. This is disrespectful of the place you are playing because it could impact his business tomorrow.

The mailing list was also a good icebreaker when trawling the bar for girls. Every stop was a hit and run with no time for small talk. You would simply tell the cute girls they could put their number down also, if they wanted. Most were flattered and they would. When you had a night off, you would just pull out the old mailing list and start making calls to hook up later.

This was a great system with only one drawback. After a busy weekend you might have a few numbers to go through. There was no way to remember who was who. And also, if you made the mistake of going around with the mailing list after a few drinks, there was no quality control. Sundays were always a surprise, never knowing who was going to open that front door. I guess it was a form of gambling, that rush when the door opens. Only seconds to decide. Do I suggest somewhere nice? Or start laying the foundation for my exit.

Frank the Bartender

One of our usual haunts was a bar called "The Baliwick". It was just a big old bar with a great crowd of regulars. Since we were there all the time we knew just about everyone. Now the title of this section is not accurate. Frank was not the bartender, he worked the door. He was a big guy that would hang at the door checking IDs and collect the cover charge. The thing that made Frank stand out from the crowd was that he had an abnormally sized manhood, enormous. And he was always pulling that thing out for no good reason. I mention this because it is an integral part of the story.

On an off night there were a few of us at the Baliwick just drinking, playing pinball and hanging out. The place was like a second home to us and the drinks were free. There was no band playing this night and the place was pretty quiet. Sometime that night three girls came into the bar that none of us recognized. And they stood out because they all looked like witches; I guess a pre-Goth kind of look. I don't know why, but Frank took an instant dislike to them. He asked the bartender what they were drinking, and ordered them a round, but asked the bartender to bring them to him first.

When the bartender dropped off the drinks, Frank unzipped under the bar, and gave each of them a good stir with little Frank. I know, that's terrible, but this was the seventies and we thought it was hilarious. When Frank was done, all three drinks were sent over, and I am pretty sure I ended up on the floor from laughing so hard.

Fear of the Dark

As most of you know, bars are not the best lit places in the world. Combining that with alcohol can be dangerous. As I said earlier, in that environment what appears to be a rare jewel may actually turn out to be a lump of charcoal in the light of day.

Case in point, a girl I will call Lizzie, as that might have been her name. By now I had become a full time crew guy and had been wise enough to become the guy that mixes the bands sound. This gave me the strategic placement of being in the audience and getting first shot before the band guys could. On this particular night I was approached by Lizzie, who had offered to buy me a drink. She was cute and buying, the perfect girl. Through the night we talked and drank and got to know each other. She was actually pretty hot, and I was looking forward to spending the rest of the evening with her.

Having made arrangements to hook up after we were done loading out, I was anxious to get finished working. After the last set the lights in the bar came up full and we started packing up while Lizzie waited. With the lights full up I thought I noticed something about her that wasn't quite right, but I couldn't figure out what.

After all the gear was loaded and we were getting ready to leave, I realized what was different. Lizzie had only one eye, and her fake one kept wandering around on its own sort of like a lizards. I have nothing against people with fake eyes, but I suddenly found myself unable to look at anything but where that eye was wandering to.

Now the thought popped in my head, exit strategy. I had to think of a way out, I couldn't spend the night with her and that lizard eye that kept wandering around. I tried to tell her that the band was having a meeting and I had to go, but while I was loading out, she was at the bar getting her nerve up with tequila. She was determined to take me home, "No" was not an option for her. And it didn't help that Al Fritsch and the rest of the band told her there was no meeting, and that we made a good looking couple. No help there. At one point she and a friend grabbed my arm and tried to physically pull me out of the bar as the band looked on and laughed hysterically.

I was no prude then, but I just couldn't get past that eye. It seemed that as the night went on, that eye was wandering more and more. Do those things get loose the longer you have them in? Also, do you keep them in when you go to bed? The thought of that thing popping out or of an empty eye socket terrified me. And the thought of an eye patch didn't help. Who wants to sleep with a pirate? The whole thing was way too much for me.

The rest of the night is a little foggy, but I do remember breaking free and running out of the bar and hiding behind my car until the coast was clear. Not my best moment.

Back then we would always meet at a diner after a gig, to sort of wind down. When I got to the diner that morning the roar of laughter that greeted me was deafening. Looking back, it was pretty funny; I just didn't think so then.

The Truck

There gets to be a time when the local bands are carrying so much equipment night to night, that many would invest in their own truck. Now as I say this, let me back up a little bit. Back in the seventies and eighties many bands were working six and seven nights a week, filling clubs that held five hundred or more. This was big business. This was back in the day of bands like The Good Rats, Zebra, Swift Kick, and Twisted Sister. But not just them, there were a lot of other bands as well. There were all types of music back then. Any night of the week there were a lot of great shows.

One particular winter night, when it came time to load out, the lock on the back of the truck was frozen solid. We couldn't get the key in to open the back up and load our gear. Now this is at five in the morning and everyone is already tired and wants to go home.

One trick is to hold a lit lighter underneath, which didn't work at all this night. The next idea would be hot water, but where do you get that at five in the morning on the sidewalk, when the club is already closed? Inspiration took hold as I stood on the back bumper and urinated on the lock. Disgusting I know, but these were desperate times. Well, that didn't work so we tried the lighter again. Held the lighter under the lock, lit it, and the lock erupted into a big fireball. I guess I drank a little too much this particular evening, as my urine turned out to be more flammable than gasoline. But the lock did open, mission accomplished.

First Time on the Road

Oddly enough, the first time I went out on the road had nothing to do with music. It was with a carnival. When I was a kid small towns used to have local fairs, in our case it was sponsored by the fire department and was known as the Annual Fireman's Fair. This was a big deal that we looked forward to all year. The fire department had a big field across the street from their station house where the carnival would set up. The fair would arrive during the week, and open on a Friday. They would be there all week and stay open for a second weekend, before packing up and moving on.

For us this was always a good time. The rides and games were always fun, and this was always a great place to meet girls that didn't go to our school. We would usually hang out all night; these fairs always took place during the summer, so nobody had to get up early the next day.

At the fair this one particular year I happened to notice the girl working the ring toss. I saw her and stopped dead in my tracks. I just thought that she was drop dead gorgeous. I was pretty sure she saw me also, so I headed over to the ring toss to say hello. Her name was Sharon, or was it Kelly? It's been a long road since then, so I'm not sure. Anyway, she was a little older than I was, hell I was a high school kid then, everyone was older.

We seemed to hit it off right away, but she was busy working so I told her that I would come back tomorrow night, which I did. I got there early, before she got busy so we could hang out and get to know each other. She was able to take a break and I think we got turkey legs for dinner. Sitting in the field at the fair, eating turkey legs with whatever her name was, I was in heaven. It was a great week; I got to see her a lot. As I said, she was older than I was and had been around the block once or twice.

As the second weekend started winding down we both knew that she would be moving on. The carnival was heading to Pittsburg for a two week run. She would be leaving and we would probably never see each other again. I went down to see her one last time and she said that we needed to talk. "Uh Oh" I thought and I got ready to run. She must have sensed this and told me not to worry, it was nothing bad.

When we were able to get a minute, she told me that she had talked to the owner of the carnival, and he said that I could stay on and come to Pittsburg and work. She seemed so happy we could stay together. Apparently no one had yet realized that I was underage. Although this was back before photo identification was a common practice. The carnival circuit at that time was filled with people working under the table for various reasons. Quite a few were on the run from the law. The carnival was the perfect place to live under the radar.

This trip to a far off land called Pittsburg sounded great to me. I had never been that far from home, so I said OK. I started working that night, learning how to dismantle the Tilt-A-Whirl, among other things. Once everything was packed up and loaded, we headed out convoy style on our long drive. Most of the rides at a carnival actually pack up and live on their own trailer so everything is really mobile. There were four of us crammed into the oversize cab of the truck, but that was fine by me. Some of the carnies used to ride in the rides that were on trailers. That would be illegal now, but back then I don't think anybody cared.

I have to admit, getting into Pittsburg the next day for the set up was exciting. These guys knew all the fairgrounds on the circuit, and each driver pulled their trailer to the spot where that ride would be set up. It was something to see these massive rides spring out of their trailers. It was kind of like those kids shows where the robots transform. I was working with the crew that put together the Tilt-A-Whirl, the Scrambler, and the Ferris Wheel.

By the end of the first day we were just about set up, even though the carnival wasn't to open for a couple of days. This gave the crew the chance to check out the rides and do a little maintenance. This also gave me a chance to spend some time with my new girlfriend. I didn't know where this was going, but I wasn't really concerned about tomorrow, today was pretty good.

A day or two into the Pittsburg run we were camped out in the haunted house after hours. Sleeping arrangements on the carnival circuit are sparse; you're kind of on your own to find a place to crash. The haunted house was covered and had ventilation. Not a bad place to spend the night. Late that night we were talking and I guess she decided to open up to me. She told me that I wasn't like the other guys she had met, I was special. On it's own that might sound nice, but she followed that with something about how she would "probably never go after me with a knife". It was the "probably" that concerned me the most.

I later found out she had gotten on the carnival circuit after an incident that involved her husband, his girlfriend, a knife and the police. As I said earlier, a lot of carnies are on the run from the law. While I lay there that night I wasn't quite sure what to do. I could tell by her breathing that she had fallen fast asleep.

It took me two days to hitch hike home from Pittsburg, and that was the last Fireman's Fair I ever went to. So much for my first road trip.

Splash

One of my first forays into the "Big Time" was with a band called Splash. At the time I was working a day job with a guy named Phil Avelli. Years before Phil had been in a band named Forest that had a minor hit. As is usually the case, things did not go as planned and Phil had to leave music to support his family. By the time I met him, years had gone by and he was attempting a comeback of sorts.

He had gotten some of the guys from his old band and put together a new band called Splash. He had also called on some of his old industry contacts to see if there was any interest. By doing this the band was able to avoid having to pound it out on the bar circuit to build a following and get a record label to look at them. Playing a showcase is when you play either a club or a rehearsal space, and have invited record people there.

Early showcases had gotten Splash a manager and a budget to record a demo. Now they were prepping for an industry showcase that would result in either a recording contract, or the end of the band. The showcase would be at The Ritz in New York City, opening 2 nights for Steele Breeze. At the time Steele Breeze had a sizeable hit with" You Don't Want Me Anymore" so the shows were a sellout.

Parts of the prep for the shows were rehearsals at S.I.R. in New York. It was, and still is, a major rehearsal venue where you are likely to run into anyone and everyone in the music business. To me, S.I.R. was exciting. People like Kiss and Alice Cooper rehearsed there.

Little did I know at the time, but in a few years I would be back at S.I.R. working with both Kiss and the Coop.

The load in at the old Ritz was amazing. The entrance was on the street, but the stage was five flights up, with no elevator. The crew that worked there would grab your road cases and run them up all five flights. These guys were something; some of the cases weighed a couple of hundred pounds. They made it look easy. This was also the first gig I ever worked that had stagehands. Up until now, at any bar I worked, I was on my own. As I said, this felt like the big time to me.

Load in went fine. Steele Breeze were first to sound check and they were cool. When they were finished we set up in front of them and did our sound check. All was good. Showtime came and Splash hit the stage with all they had. They came off well and did a really good job. This gig was for all the marbles and they knew it. The show on the second night went equally as well. Now it was time for the waiting game. It would be at least a few days before the bands manager heard from all the record companies about a potential deal. This was an important time for me, if Splash got signed I would be working on the record and go out on my first tour.

As the week went by, one by one all the record companies passed on Splash. They all agreed the band was good, but they just weren't interested. At this point, with no deal in sight, the guys disbanded. Once again I was out of a gig. So close, but not close enough.

Getting Serious

After a few years of knocking around the club circuit setting up big light shows, sound systems, backdrops and band gear I was exhausted. Back then you would get to a club between 4 and 6 p.m. and not get finished until about 5 a.m. But while I was working nights in rock and roll; I also kept a day job. It had been drummed into me at an early age that you had to have a job you can count on. And at this stage rock and roll was far from reliable.

What this meant was that I would get home from a gig usually about six in the morning and would have to be to work by eight. That left me about an hour and a half to shower and sleep before I had to go do it all over again. Day job from eight until five, and then go straight to the club until five the next morning. I would do this four to five days a week and catch up on sleep on Sunday. It was common for me to wake up on the toilet in my bathroom after a gig. I would get home tired, go to use the toilet and fall asleep in about a minute. When I would wake up an hour or so later I would go to stand and fall to the floor, as lack of circulation from sitting so long had put both my legs to sleep. More than one morning was spent flapping around on my bathroom floor, like a fish in the bottom of a boat, until the feeling in my legs returned.

At any rate, that is where I was when I decided to give up doing shows. I was tired and felt I was going nowhere, so I walked away. Finally, I had enough rest, and I had my life back. No more working all the time. If there has ever been a year in my life I have wasted, it was that one. I was lost, bored and found myself gravitating back to the clubs I had walked away from. I think that doing shows is somehow in my blood. There was no walking away, although I tried.

The boredom I was experiencing led to frustration, which led to drinking a lot more than I should have. Although in this instance it may have been a benefit. Even though I missed doing shows, I was still gun shy about going back. I had been offered gigs here and there, but had always turned them down. One night I went to a club called "The Starship" to see a band that was very big at the time, The Kut, and proceeded to drink myself blind. After the first set I ran into an old friend, Raymie, who was working for the band that night. We had worked together for years and had become good friends. It turned out The Kut needed another tech, and while under the influence of way too much booze, Raymie recruited me and I agreed. Had I been sober I more than likely would never have said yes, so I guess my lack of sobriety that night was a blessing in disguise.

Looking back it is amazing that the band hired me. When Raymie took me into the dressing room so they could meet the new crew guy, I was so drunk I could barely stand. The guys in the band didn't bat an eye, and for that I am thankful. John, Tommy and John, I owe you more than you know. In retrospect, getting that gig saved my life and gave me a purpose. I suspect if I had stayed on the path I was on, things would have gone bad sooner or later. The reason that this section is called getting serious is that it was at this time in my life I realized that music was my future, so I better get it together.

The Next Level

The Kut were one of the bigger bands in my area so
working for them was the big time in the local scene.
I did take things more seriously and it is at this point I
learned a level of professionalism that carried me
through most of my career. These guys had been on
the circuit a while, and they were highly regarded. By
working with them I got into a circle of people that
were taking it to the next level professionally.

Working with The Kut I met a lot of other bands, and
their crews. Bands like Cintron and Ruffkut gave me
an opportunity to broaden my working knowledge,
and continue to network with other people in the
industry. As I was to find out, networking can mean
the difference between working and not working.
There are a lot of talented people out there, but if no
one knows who you are, it won't matter.

During this period I was working a lot, but the gigs
were enjoyable to the point I didn't mind the fatigue
that came with it. We were playing in a lot of clubs I
had never seen before, and by working with different
bands and crews, it never got dull. Whether I was
loading in to "L'Amour" in Brooklyn with Ruffkut or
"Cheers" with Cintron, I was having a great time and
learning new skills that would serve me well in the
years to come. Again, I had also made a few more
lifelong friends with this new group I was working
with.

These three bands formed the core of my experience
at the time. The Kut were a three-piece heavy metal
band that just exploded on stage every night. Guitar,
bass and drums, both guys up front sang. John Miceli,

John Roggio and Tommy Henriksen were all great musicians. The Kut was a band I used to pay to go see, so to me these shows weren't work at all.

Cintron was fronted by George Cintron. George was an incredible singer and an incredible guitarist, along with being a gifted songwriter. The fact that he could do all that made for a show you would not forget. This was another band I used to pay to see. Working for George was especially rewarding in that one of his songs was the song my wife and I picked out years later for our wedding.

Ruffkut was also an experience. Members of that band and The Kut had been in bands together over the years, so everyone, including the crews, were old friends. A lot of these guys are like brothers to me. A few have gone on to some of the biggest tours in the world, some have left the business and have gone into other things. But the great thing about it is that none of that mattered, everyone has stayed close. When I was on tour with Kiss, if I got home on a break I would head straight to the local rock clubs where I grew up. Often I would do gigs with local bands, for free if they couldn't afford a crew. Those clubs were like my second home and I loved every minute of it. I go back every chance I get. Whenever I go to a show, I always end up on the loading dock hanging out with the crew. That feels like home too.

Brothers

The name of this book is "We" are the road crew after all, so maybe it's time to talk about some of the crew guys I started out with. These guys were there at the beginning, and will always be like brothers. They are Raymie, Todd, Howie, Vinnie, Charlie, Ralph and Blake. We were working together when none of us had a nickel to our names, and our futures were definitely uncertain. But through it all we remained tight. From bar gigs where some of us didn't have gas money to get home, to some of the biggest shows all over the world. These are the people that will always look after you. I have always believed that the friends you have when you have nothing are the only friends you can ever be sure of. I will list these guys and give them each their credit, as they have all done much and made me proud.

Raymie: The person responsible for getting me back in the business is still out on the road somewhere. He has continued to get consistent work touring. He has been a guitar and drum tech, and has also worked a lot of different production jobs. Wherever he is, it is usually where he wants to be. And not only has he had a successful career, but for some unknown reason he doesn't age. He looks the same as the day I met him in college over twenty five years ago. Our meeting in college is also a good story. Back then we were the only two long haired guitar carrying guys in the student union. I don't know why, but we just started hanging out and became friends. Years later when I asked Raymie how we hooked up, he put it simply, "no one else was going to hang out with either one of us, so we had to become friends". I guess he was right.

Todd: Todd was a drum tech when I met him, just a kid. Through the years he has grown into a seasoned professional. He has gone on to Production Manage and Tour Manage some of the biggest tours in the past few years. Over the years he and I, on more than one occasion, were able to help keep the other employed. That's how you survive in the business, having people in your life that have your back.

Howie: Howie came along later, he started coming to shows we were working and realized it was what he wanted to do. He caught on fast and it wasn't long before he was getting gigs on his own. Howie went as far as he wanted in the touring business and left it some years ago. He is currently a very happy and very successful businessman in Arizona.

Vinnie: Vinnie was and is the front of house sound man. It is a job he is good at, probably one of the best in the business. He continues to work steadily and can be found at the mixing desk on tours all over the world.

Charlie: When I first met Charlie he had already been out on the road. That placed him well ahead of the rest of us. Charlie was and is a backline guy, doing just about any instrument on a tour. He has consistently worked through the years, and can also be found on tours all over the world.

A funny story about a club gig I did with Charlie, we were driving home after a really long and late load out and we were both exhausted. Charlie volunteered to drive the truck, which was great, I was wiped out. I started to doze off in the front of the truck and it wasn't long before I was roused by the honking of our horn. I woke up and saw Charlie passed out asleep sprawled across the steering wheel; the weight of his body was the only thing keeping us in a straight line. After a pit stop for coffee we were fine, but that story will always live on.

Ralph: Ralph was primarily a lighting guy, but he got his first break as a drum tech. I worked with him a lot over the years, and you will see his name throughout these pages. He left the road some time ago and now owns and operates his own company.

Blake: When I first met Blake he was just a guy that came to shows and hung out. Most of us got to be friends with him. It wasn't long before he figured out he wanted to do lights. To his credit, he learned everything he could and took any gig. If there was a seminar or class, he took it. He worked really hard and got good at what he wanted to do. He has worked on Broadway, toured continually, and has been in charge of one of the larger concert venues back in New York. All of this was done by hard work and determination.

That I have chosen to list these guys should in no way infer that these were the only people I worked with. There are too many good people to list. It's just that these guys are the stand outs, the brothers on the road. There are certain people in your life that you have so much history with, you can't imagine a life that doesn't include them.

Moving Forward

The experience I got while working the circuit led me to the next level of bands. When you use the term "National" it usually means that the band is known around the country and probably has a record out. Getting to work with a national act is an important stepping stone.

For me things happened close together. John Miceli, the drummer from The Kut, got a gig playing with Talas, definitely a national act. At the same time Tommy Henriksen, the bass player from The Kut, got a gig with a band called Heaven. Both guys brought me with them and these gigs were a sizable step up for me. Talas was the band Billy Sheehan was in before he got in David Lee Roth's band. They were well known, had records out, and were also a great live band. They were playing rooms I had never worked before and they were selling out. By the time I started working for them the only original member was the singer, but it still turned out to be an opportunity that would boost my career in ways I never could have known.

The other band I was working with, Heaven, had scored a hit with a song called "Rock School", they were actually international. Heaven had toured around the world, although my work with them never took me outside New York. They were also playing bigger rooms than I had been in before. It seemed like my career was finally starting to go somewhere.

Now that I had two bands of notoriety that I was working with, and things were moving right along, it seems only natural what happened next. Talas broke up, and Heaven stopped playing, for some unknown reason. I guess the roller coaster that was my career had hit the top of the hill and was about to plummet straight down. I wondered if the carnival still had openings.

Heavy Metal All Stars

After the Talas gigs I was asked by the guitar player, Al Pitrelli, to do a show at "L'Amour" in Queens. The show was the Heavy Metal All Stars which included Al, Dave Spitz on bass; he had been playing with Black Sabbath. Also in the band were A.J. Pero from Twisted Sister and Rhett Forrester, the old singer from Riot. It turned out to be a good gig with a packed house. L'Amour was one of the bigger clubs around. The show was great, good musicians playing great rock songs. I'm still glad I did that gig. All the guys were cool to work with.

There were two things about that night that have always stayed with me. Before the show, in the dressing room when Rhett changed his shirt you could see he had serious scars all over. When one of the guys asked him about them, he started pointing to them one by one and telling the story that went with each knife and gunshot wound. I believed every word; I could tell Rhett was not the type to walk away from a fight, which leads me to story number two from that night.

One of our friends, Mike, had been hitting on a girl at the bar, and her boyfriend had gotten jealous. He and his friends were going to kick Mike's ass. He asked a few of us to walk him out of the bar, which Rhett and a few of us volunteered to do. Now the point was to avoid a fight, but as soon as we got near those other guys Rhett started yelling at them, calling them pansies, fags, you name it. You could tell he wanted nothing more than to take them all on. I don't have a doubt in my mind he could have kicked all their asses by himself; he just had that way about him. I think the guys at the bar saw that too, they backed off and our friend Mike was able to get out safely.

That turned out to be the only show I would ever do with Rhett. He was shot to death a few years later. If you get the chance, try to do a web search on him. Some of his music is still available.

Ramones

I used to stagehand at all the clubs in my area where there was work. It would consist of load in and load out, and whatever the bands crew needed, whether it was help with gear, running lights, running spotlight, and anything else you could think of. When I heard The Ramones were going to play one of the clubs I worked at, I made sure I was on that crew call.

I had always been a big Ramones fan, so the thought of doing this gig, and possibly meeting them, was a big deal to me. I got to load in early; I wanted to make sure I didn't miss anything. When the Ramones crew got there, we unloaded sound, lights, and backline, and started setting up. As a stagehand you are there to set up anything and everything that the band needs. Sound check was going to be around six, and I heard that the band would be there for it, and they were. I got to meet them one by one and they were all pretty cool guys. After sound check the Ramones lighting guy said he needed two guys to work the show running spotlights for the band. I volunteered right away.

In an arena spotlights are placed in secure areas away from the crowd, as they are not only important to the show, but they tend to get hot, really hot. So safety is an issue. Now this club didn't really have anywhere to put these enormous lights, so the Ramones crew put a road case by either side of the soundboard, laid them on their side, off their wheels, and put the spotlights up there. They told us there would be enough room to stand up there as well, and run the light.

Before the show the lighting guy gave each of us a headset so that he could tell us what he wanted us to do. Just before the show we climbed up onto these road cases, fired up the lights, and held on for dear life. This club was packed to the walls with fans that were going wild. They were jammed up against my road case so tight I couldn't have fallen off if I tried.

It wasn't long before things got so crazy that my entire road case with me and my light started moving. The lighting guy was yelling at me to stay on Joey the singer, but my case was being shoved around the club ten feet in any direction. I couldn't focus on anything, I was just trying to hold on and not get burned. I'm pretty sure that my spotlight did shine in the area of the band a few times that night, so it wasn't a total waste.

After the show I figured I was just going to get fired off the gig right then and there. I was sure that the lighting guy was going to be pissed off at me for screwing up. When the club finally emptied out to a point where we could start working, I went over toward the lighting guy to take the hit. I figured I would just get it over with. When I got there he was laughing so hard he couldn't talk. It turned out this sort of thing was a regular occurrence at their shows. There really wasn't any other way for them to run spotlights at their gigs, so they just did what they could and laughed at the local crew guys later. Lesson learned, and I still had any amazing time that night.

Out of the Blue

By this time I had no steady gigs booked, and there was nothing going on, no future potential for any gigs. Some of the guys from Talas had formed a new band called Danger Danger, and I did a couple of shows with them, but they were few and far between. They were concentrating more on song writing and getting a record deal. Life can be funny; just when you think you are completely down and out, things can turn completely around.

A friend of mine that we all called Pugsly had been working for a local drummer named Lou Appel for years. Lou was working a lot and playing with a lot of different people. At this time he was playing with a new singer named Debbie Gibson. Debbie had songs on the charts, but was still in high school. Because of this they couldn't tour, and only played weekends. Mostly college auditoriums which were actually big concert halls. Anyway, Pugsly had just gotten a tour with a band called White Lion, so he asked me if I wanted the Gibson gig. Of course I said yes, even though I wasn't sure I wanted the gig. I figured I could check it out and if I didn't like it, I could bail.

My first day on this new gig was at a local rehearsal studio, not far from where I lived. This was my first clue that this gig was a step up; we got paid to rehearse and work on gear. I had never had that before. We rehearsed a couple of times a week, then packed the gear in a truck and did our weekend gigs. This was a lot more civilized than I had ever had it before. My first meeting with the band and crew went really well. I had been apprehensive about this job from the beginning. This was a whole new circle of people that I had to work with and prove myself to. And this was not exactly my kind of music. But as it turned out the people were great and the gig was one I was actually lucky to have gotten.

I would be working with Adam the percussionist and Louie the drummer. Until this point I had mainly been a guitar tech that could set up the drums. This gig had a lot more to it than I had done before. The guys were actually very cool and showed me what I needed to know. I caught on fast and things went smoothly. It was at this time I met John Karlquist who was doing guitars and keyboards. As the years went on he and I became good friends and did a lot of tours together.

After the first few rehearsals I got to know Debbie and her family. Her career was a family business, and everyone did what they could to help. Her Mom Diane managed her, and her Grandmother used to cut our paychecks. This made for a good atmosphere to start my new job in. As the years went on I continued to work on and off for the Gibson's, and in all that time their change from working class people to multi platinum artist, they never changed. At least not in the way they treated me.

After the first week of rehearsals it was off to my first gig. We were playing a college in upstate New York, which I had never done before. I was more used to working the seedy rock clubs in the towns we went to. When we got to the gig I saw that it would hold about three thousand. I had never done anything this big before. Not only that, the opening act was on at seven thirty and we were on at nine. This was a lot earlier than I was used to going on. I could actually get home at a decent hour. The load in and set up were great, we had college stage hands and there was plenty of room to work. This new gig was working out better than I could have hoped. It also had included something I had never seen before, catering. When we got to the gigs there was lunch and dinner there for us. More and more I knew that all my years knocking around the clubs had finally paid off.

The first show I did with Debbie and her band was also a culture shock. We had done sound check and everything was fine. When show time came, all the performers came out of the dressing rooms and waited behind the stage. When the lights went out the roar of three thousand fans was deafening. It gave me chills. Everyone took the stage and the show went off perfectly. The load out went great and as predicted, I was in bed at a time I would normally have been tuning guitars in a rock club. All in all, a good first show.

The schedule of rehearsing during the week and doing shows on the weekends continued to go well. There was starting to be talk of a summer tour when Debbie graduated high school. Since her album was high on the charts, I was not surprised. As the weeks went by, the tour plans actually started to take shape. But before that would happen, we found out about a very big show we would be doing in a couple of weeks, the Atlantic Records Fortieth birthday party at Madison Square Garden.

The Big One

The Atlantic Records birthday party performance was not only going to take place at Madison Square Garden, it was going to be broadcast live on HBO. After all was said and done, I was told that over forty million people had tuned in. Some of the other artists on the bill were Genesis and the surviving members of Led Zeppelin. This show was going to be huge.

We showed up at this massive arena with our little truck full of band gear. Surrounding us were the tractor trailers of some of the other groups. As if Madison Square Garden wasn't intimidating enough. We were quickly shown by the production team where to unload our gear and what to do.

As there were many groups on this bill we would have to get our gear onstage quickly and go. We preset what we could and when the time came the stagehands just grabbed our gear and off we went. The band played their set and it all went pretty well. When they were done our gear was unceremoniously tossed off the stage so the next group could go. While we were packing up I think both John and I felt a sense of relief that it was over.

Normally we would have had to wait to bring our truck in and load up, but as things were so crowded backstage we were told to go ahead, but be quick. As John was backing our truck up to load out, I heard a few of the production team start to yell for him to stop. Apparently he nearly ran over Phil Collins as he was walking toward the stage. I guess Phil doesn't normally have trucks careening toward him backstage, so he was caught a bit off guard.

Sea World

Another of our gigs before the tour was a trip to Florida to play at Sea World. After Florida we would be driving the truck to North Dakota to play for some contest winners, and then home to New York. After rehearsal we loaded the truck to get ready, but we weren't leaving until morning, as it was a long drive.

I had never been to Florida before, so I was looking forward to this trip. John and I had a twenty-four foot rental truck with all our band gear and sound equipment. We headed out early to get a good start. The plan was to drive most of the way there, get a hotel, and finish the next day.

We were less than a hundred miles out when the truck started to make noises. The noises turned to vibrations which finally got so bad we couldn't drive the truck. We were stuck at a gas station. Eventually we were able to rent another truck, but we still had to unload the whole truck at the gas station, and pack everything into the new truck. It had taken hours to get the second truck, and even more time to reload the equipment. Now we would have to drive straight through and take turns driving while the other guy tried to sleep.

We got to our hotel at Sea World the night before the gig, so the show would not be delayed. The next morning we loaded in and did the show, loaded out, and went to the hotel to collapse before our drive to North Dakota. The rest of the trip went fine, but we sure did log a lot of miles, good practice for what was to come.

Standard opening pages for a crew itinerary

BEFORE WE START THIS TOUR THERE ARE A FEW THINGS THAT THOSE OF US IN UPPER LOWER MANAGEMENT (OR IS IT LOWER-MIDDLE MANAGEMENT?) WOULD LIKE YOU TO KNOW.

WE ARE LOOKING FORWARD TO WORKING WITH YOU AND THE FOLLOWING SET OF GUIDELINES WILL HELP ESTABLISH TOUR POLICY AND HELP US ALL WORK TOWARD A COMMON GOAL OF A SMOOTH RUNNING, SUCCESSFUL TOUR.

ALL THE INFORMATION CONTAINED HERE WAS BELIEVED TO BE CORRECT WHEN THESE ITINERARIES WERE PRINTED. WHEREVER TELEPHONE NUMBERS OR SCHEDULES WERE UNAVAILABLE THEY ARE NOTED WITH "TBA". WE WILL GET YOU THE ADDITIONAL AND/OR CORRECTED INFO AS SOON AS WE GET IT.

LAMINATED PASSES WILL BE ISSUED TO EVERYONE WORKING ON THE TOUR. THESE PASSES ARE FOR YOUR OWN USE ONLY AND SHOULD NOT BE GIVEN AWAY TO ANYONE FOR THE PURPOSE OF GAINING ACCESS TO A VENUE OR A BACKSTAGE AREA. ALL PASSES WILL BE NUMBERED. ANYONE WHO IS SEEN WEARING A LAMINATED PASS AND IS UNKNOWN TO US WILL BE STOPPED ON SIGHT, THE PASS WILL BE TAKEN OFF THEM AND THEY WILL BE ESCORTED FROM THE BACKSTAGE AND THE BUILDING. THE NUMBERING SYSTEM WILL THEN INDICATE WHERE THE PASS CAME FROM.

ALL GUESTS WILL BE ISSUED DAY OF SHOW PASSES. PLEASE ADVISE YOUR GUESTS THAT A GUEST PASS DOES NOT ALLOW THEM TO PHOTOGRAPH THE SHOW.

ALL GUEST LISTS WILL BE CLOSED AT 2:30 PM ON SHOW DAYS OR WHEN THE ALLOTMENT IS USED UP. WE HAVE A LIMITED NUMBER OF TICKETS IN EACH VENUE SO DON'T FEEL OBLIGATED TO INVITE EVERYONE YOU'VE MET IN THE AIRPORT, HOTEL, TENNIS COURT OR CHURCH OF YOUR CHOICE. PLEASE NOTE THAT IN THE MAJORITY OF TOUR VENUES, GUESTS MUST HAVE A TICKET AS WELL AS A PASS IN ORDER TO GAIN ACCESS TO THE VENUE SEATING AREA.

GUESTS SHOULD NOT BE IN THE BACKSTAGE AREAS FROM FIFTEEN (15) MINUTES PRIOR TO THE SHOW, DURING THE SHOW AND UNTIL FIFTEEN (15) MINUTES AFTER EACH BAND'S SHOW ENDS.

DRESSING ROOM AND STAGE ACCESS WILL BE RESTRICTED TO ONLY NECESSARY PERSONS DURING TIMES OF EACH BAND'S PERFORMANCE. THERE WILL BE A CODING SYSTEM TO ALLOW FOR IDENTIFICATION. DETAILS TO FOLLOW AT A LATER TIME.

Continued.

EVERYONE'S TIME IS VALUABLE. PLEASE BE ON TIME FOR ALL HOTEL, VENUE AND AIRPORT DEPARTURES OR YOU WILL GET LEFT BEHIND. YOU ARE RESPONSIBLE FOR YOUR WAKE-UP CALLS IN HOTELS. PLEASE USE A TRAVEL ALARM CLOCK AND WEAR A WATCH.

PLEASE MAKE SURE YOU PAY YOUR PERSONAL HOTEL CHARGES AT LEAST THIRTY (30) MINUTES PRIOR TO DEPARTURE TIME, AND REMEMBER, THERE COULD BE LONG LINES AT CHECKOUT. NEVER CHARGE ITEMS TO YOUR ROOM AFTER YOU HAVE CHECKED OUT. ALWAYS KEEP YOUR RECEIPTS EVEN IF IT IS A ZERO-BALANCE SHOWING NO CHARGES. FAILURE TO PAY YOUR INCIDENTALS WILL RESULT IN A SURCHARGE. IF YOU EVER HAVE ANY PROBLEMS WITH HOTELS ALONG THE TOUR TELL ME OR YOUR TOUR MANAGER.

YOU WILL RECEIVE A WEEKLY PER DIEM AT THE BEGINNING OF EVERY WEEK. SHOULD THIS PROVE INSUFFICIENT, YOU SHOULD CARRY CREDIT CARDS. THERE WILL BE NO SALARY ADVANCES ON THE ROAD.

HOT MEALS AT SHOWS AND FOOD AND DRINK ARE PROVIDED FOR PEOPLE WORKING ON THE TOUR AND SHOULD NOT BE TREATED AS A RESTAURANT/BAR SERVICE FOR GUESTS WHICH COULD LEAD TO PEOPLE WHO ARE BUSY AT MEAL TIMES GOING WITHOUT.

THE PRODUCTION OFFICE IS A PLACE OF OFFICIAL TOUR BUSINESS AND NOT A LOUNGE. TELEPHONES ARE FOR PRODUCTION RELATED CALLS ONLY, NO PERSONAL TELEPHONE CALLS AND PLEASE REMEMBER PRODUCTION RUNNERS ARE NOT FOR PERSONAL USE.

WE WILL ATTEMPT TO HAVE A LAUNDRY RUN EVERY SHOW DAY. DEADLINE FOR DROPOFF WILL BE POSTED OUTSIDE THE PRODUCTION OFFICE. YOUR NAME MUST BE MARKED ON THE BAG (S) AND YOU ARE REQUIRED TO PREPAY FOR THE SERVICE. THE RECEIPT AND ANY CHANGE WILL BE RETURNED WITH YOUR CLEAN CLOTHES.

THANK YOU IN ADVANCE FOR YOUR COOPERATION.

The rules of conduct

On the Road

We set out on the first tour not long after Debbie graduated high school. This was a much anticipated tour, as she had had several singles on the charts. We would be taking out full production, sound, lights, a stage set, and backline. This was the real deal. We would be playing a lot of outdoor amphitheaters, called sheds, which were great venues with a lot of room to work.

Pre production and rehearsals would be at an arena in Massachusetts, which was also our first gig. John and I took the old truck out for one last spin; we would drive to the arena and drop off the truck. From here on our gear would be riding in the tractor trailers with the rest of the gear. No more driving gig to gig, we would be on a tour bus, which was also something new to me.

When we loaded into the first arena it seemed enormous. With the sound and lights, and also the stage set, it seemed like too much. At one point I actually got nervous, as I felt a little out of my league. I was a sandlot player trying out for the major leagues. It's funny now, but at the time I really had my doubts. I talked to Louie the drummer about it and I'm pretty sure he said something along the line of "Relax; stop acting so stupid, it will be fine". Probably some of the best advice I have had so far. The rehearsals went OK and so did the first show. Now I was in the major leagues and I felt like I belonged. It also felt good to not have to drive the truck after the gig. It was nice getting on the tour bus, eating pizza and crashing in my bunk.

The tour rolled along, city to city and I got to start seeing parts of the country I had never been to. I also started to make new friends with the rest of the crew. As we were all on the same bus, living and working together, it was inevitable. I haven't kept in touch with many of them, but our house sound mixer, Steve Botting, has become a good friend. I have had the good fortune of working with him many times.

This whole concept of catering at the gigs, hotels on days off, per diem, and the swag were all still new to me. I felt fortunate and was glad I decided to stick it out. Per Diem is the cash they give you on the road so you don't need to touch your paycheck. Never mind the paycheck, the per diem alone was more than I was used to making. And I still couldn't believe what I was making in my check, which went straight home. Swag is the free t shirts that promoters and vendors give you, for no reason at all. Every day was like Christmas. People would just show up and give you stuff. I know it sounds corny but I will repeat myself, I felt fortunate that I had decided to stick it out.

There were plenty of club gigs I had done where there was little or no money. Starting out I had to ride my bicycle to gigs no matter how far it was. There were nights we were loading into clubs, in the rain. Nights the truck broke down and it took hours to get home. No room to work properly. Times we had to carry our stuff out through the crowd. We never got fed, and sometimes there was nothing nearby. You just had to do the gig and hope to eat later. While I was still amazed and thankful for my new found good fortune, I always remembered where I came from. I think that has always kept me grounded. This is not a job, it is who you are.

The Bus

Part of life on a tour like this was the tour bus. These are usually custom coaches that can house twelve or more people comfortably. I was amazed when I first got on. The front section was a full lounge complete with couches, stereo, kitchen area, television and VCR, even a small bathroom. The center section is where the bunks are located, bunk alley. Most buses I have been on have the bunks three high and have had twelve bunks. They are small, but comfortable once you get used to them. The back of the bus also had a lounge with couches, cooler, television, etc. For a guy who was used to getting a little sleep in the truck, this was paradise. Once you get used to bus life, it is actually comfortable and enjoyable.

After a gig there were always facilities to clean up and shower. When load out is done, time to shower up and head out to the bus for pizza and beer. You see while we were working those same people that always gave us free stuff would stock the bus with cold beer and hot food for after the show. The bus truly becomes your home away from home. Also, a quick word about the bathroom on the bus, VERY IMPORTANT! The toilet is for number one only. The bus toilet flushes into a holding tank that needs to be emptied periodically. If number two is put into the holding tank it will smell up the bus for the entire drive. The bus driver will usually have to stop and have the holding tank emptied, and if the offending party is caught, not only will he get an ass kicking; the bus driver will make him pay for the dumping of the tank.

A funny story relating to bus toilets, one of my oldest friends on the road had to go really bad. He had eaten a lot of Chinese food and it wasn't sitting too well. By the time he had his emergency the bus was driving through the desert with nowhere to stop. The driver was not about to turn the bus around, he had a long drive and needed to be on time. They say that necessity is the mother of invention, but I think that desperation can get the ideas moving a lot quicker. My buddy realized he was in trouble, big trouble. Inspiration took hold after seeing one of the garbage bags in the kitchen area. He took the bag into the bathroom and lined the toilet with it. Essentially he was just going in the bag. Finally relieved he finished his business, cleaned up, secured the bag with a good sturdy knot and emerged from the bathroom triumphantly. He then proceeded to run through the lounge with this ten pound bag of volcanic lava, and head for the door to dispose of it.

While the bus was rolling down the interstate at eighty miles an hour he opened the front door and heaved his parcel of doom as hard as he could. Funny thing about a bus going eighty miles an hour though, the buses forward speed creates a resistance equal to the speed. You actually have eighty mile an hour winds buffeting you. What my friend had done was hurl his parcel into a hurricane that was blowing straight at him. Needless to say the wind took the bag and sent it right back at the side of the bus, where it caught on a rivet and tore open. From inside the bus it appeared that the windows had instantly been painted black. And it wasn't long before it started to smell. Did I mention the bus was driving through the desert? That stuff baked on for nine hours, and he spent the next day, all day cleaning the side of the bus.

Typical Day on the Road

I am often reminded of something my first production manager Omar once said when asked about days on the road. He said, "If you wake up outside a concrete building, it's a gig day, if you wake up in a hotel parking lot, it's a day off". I didn't get it then, but in time I saw the wisdom in those words. On the road time is irrelevant. You may work twelve days in a row; you may have three days off. Weekends and any sense of structure do not exist. The local newspaper in catering becomes your lifeline to the world.

It isn't long before the days on a tour become routine. If I woke up in my bunk and looked out and saw a concrete building, I would get dressed and go find catering and eat. Before long it's time to dump your semi and start working on your gear. Band gear is usually last to hit the stage, so you wait around a lot. Sound check is almost always at four, and dinner is usually at six. After dinner do your last pre show checks. Start the show at nine, finish by eleven. Load out, shower and be on the bus eating pizza by twelve thirty. You get a routine as most people do, just a much different routine.

The rest of the crew each had their own schedule as well. Typically the Production Manager and Stage Manager, along with the Riggers would be first in the building. The Production Manager would set up his office and set about his days work. He would be in charge of the big picture, making sure all the elements were there. He would also advance upcoming shows on the tour. He would coordinate with the local promoters and make sure they understood the scope of what we needed when we came to town.

The Stage Manager would be out on the floor working with the road crew and the local crew provided by the promoter. He would make sure that each department got the help they needed to do their job. He would also let each department know when and where they could dump their truck, and when they could take the stage. As each department is hustling to get their job done, the Stage Manager keeps order and makes sure there is no friction. Come show time he will often give the band and crew the countdown until show begins. You can often hear him bellowing down the halls," Ten Minutes, Ten Minutes". He also runs the load out as he did the load in.

Let's not forget the truck drivers, the guys that got our gear there. These guys are the backbone of a tour. They drive amazing distances in short amounts of time to make sure load in does not start late. These guys are some of the best there are at what they do. Some gigs have loading docks with approaches that are so difficult that an ordinary experienced truck driver would say that it was impossible. I have seen some of these touring truck drivers back in to places that most people would have trouble getting their car in to. These guys are really the first in, since they have been working since last nights load out. A good truck driver can make or break a load in.

The Riggers are the other members of the crew that are first in. These are the guys that figure out how and where to hang the bands equipment from the steel supports of the buildings roof. They calculate the loads, figure out placement, and climb up into the steel to make it happen. It is not unusual for these guys to spend their day over a hundred feet in the air.

Next in would typically be the light crew and sound crew. They get their equipment placed and fly out all that they need. At this point the carpenters would take over and start building the stage set and barricade. These days stage sets tend to be big, so this can sometimes be like building a house. When the carpenters are done, sound and lights will place what they need on stage, and pyro will start to set their effects. It is at this point backline, or band gear would get to work setting up the bands instruments.

After a few days of this, dates and calendars lose all meaning. Signs are posted all over the gig letting you know work times, meal times, sound check and show times. But just as importantly, they tell you what day it is and where you are, and also where you will be tomorrow. When the days all blur together it is common to lose track of these basic things.

Hello Cleveland

If you get the chance, watch the movie "Spinal Tap". After having been on the road I think that it is not only hilarious, but it also accurately portrays some of the crazy things that can go wrong while doing shows. I have had more than my share of Spinal Tap moments, some of which you will see in this book.

When the stage was built for the Gibson tour, there was no provision made for a tech to leave the drum riser without going on stage. Behind the riser were raised deck structures that had cross bracing underneath, which was directly behind the riser. If the drummer needed something during the show, I had to climb through all the bracing to get it, and it took a while. When the show was ready to start, Louie would announce the band" All right (insert city name here) would you please welcome…Debbie Gibson. Louie had a deep booming voice and he was perfect for this. He would use one of the backup singers' microphones and when he was done I would run it over to her.

Our Spinal Tap night began like every other, we were set to go, the band started playing. Louie was getting ready to announce the band when he looked at me and asked where are we? I looked back at him blankly, I couldn't remember. I went under the stage as fast as I could to find out. The band had started and the show was waiting on this announcement. No one that I asked knew where we were. I ran to my work box and checked my itinerary, found it, ran back, climbed under the stage. Louie made the announcement and we started the show. That was probably two minutes, but they were a long two minutes.

End of the First Tour

We spent the entire summer traveling around the U.S. and Canada, and I was glad that I had gotten to go. I already knew how unstable the music business was, and I realized that when I got home I could end up scrapping around the clubs again looking for work. I had already let the crew I was working with know I was looking for my next gig; hopefully one of them would end up on a tour that needed someone.

The tour finished in early September, and just as we started out, John and I ended up back in the truck with the band gear returning it to all the musicians. The tour was officially done and Debbie would be working on her next record before she did any shows. The Gibson's did need help here and there so I was able to get some day work, which helped.

I also did end up back in the clubs, there was a lot of regular crew work, and there were some guitar tech gigs. Between what I saved from the tour and the work I could scrape up, I got by. But you are only as good as your last gig, and I knew I needed another tour to keep my career moving forward. I made a lot of phone calls and even checked out artist management companies from the back of CD's so I could send out resumes. Resumes, by the way, will never get you a gig. Your reputation on the road is what will get you work. You can be the best tech in the world, but if you're a jerk to live with, nobody will want you. You need to be good at your gig and work and play well with others. The bus is too cramped a space for idiots.

All Out of Love (And Money)

As the title suggests, it doesn't take long for the money to run out. I had been home a little while and was going slowly broke. I had even contemplated going back to getting a regular job, giving up. Earlier I said something about the importance of friends to help get you your next job. It was at this juncture that this was illustrated to me in a big way.

I got a call from Steve Botting, a friend from the Gibson tour. He possibly had work and wanted to know if I was interested. Of course I was. He explained to me that Air Supply needed a crew and he thought he could get me and John Karlquist the gig. There would be a few details to work out if we took the job. The band was rehearsing in Los Angeles and was looking for an L.A. crew so they could save on expenses. As they had no luck finding someone, Steve proposed a deal with them. They would pay the airfare to L.A., John and I would find a place to stay, and they would pay for a rental car. This is not normal in the business, and was the only time I ever did a deal like that. But when you are starting out and don't yet have the reputation to get work, you do what you have to do. It's called paying dues.

The deal was done and we were on our way to L.A. for our second tour. Steve had made the arrangements for a car, and had found us a place to live. We would be staying at the Franklin Plaza Suites in Hollywood. They were furnished efficiencies with kitchens. And the place was not expensive. In the years to come I ended up living there quite often and actually felt at home there. All in all this was an exciting time.

Living in L.A and working for a well known band. It all worked out fine and the guys turned out to be great to work for. Once again I felt very lucky. Also as I am a big fan of old movies, the chance to check out the used book stores and all the old memorabilia places were great. We would rehearse for two weeks in California before we went to Japan. After Japan we would play Taiwan, The Philippines, then the States and finally South America. With the exception of the States I had not yet been to any of these places, so this would be a great trip. The rehearsal schedule was easy and the rest of the crew, which was small, was also really cool.

It was at this time, I am sad to say, that the Emperor of Japan died. This was a loss to the world, but in Japan this was devastating. The entire country went into mourning. This turn of events caused the cancellation of our shows in Japan. A lot of things were cancelled there out of respect. There was talk that the shows might be rescheduled, but they never were. We would be delayed in leaving, and we would just go straight to Taiwan as that was scheduled.

As we were delayed and had to stay in L.A. longer than originally scheduled, John and I needed to do a little renegotiating, we had only agreed to put ourselves up for two weeks. This delay wasn't coming out of our pockets. We spoke to the Tour Manager, Bernie Boyle about our issues. To our surprise he and the band agreed. All was taken care of and we had a couple of free days in California. The old Hollywood homes of the stars were amazing to see, and I checked out as much Hollywood movie history as I could.

Taiwan

The flight to Taiwan was a long one, the longest I had been on so far. Not that I had flown all that much, most of my miles were on the ground. This was also my first time dealing with customs and immigration. It took a lot of paperwork to get into a country, although these days it is much more difficult. We were picked up at the airport and taken to our hotel. The long flight and time change had taken its toll. We had the day off to do whatever we wanted so after a quick shower it was off to see what we could see.

We were in Taipei, the capital city of Taiwan. That evening the mayor and some aides were hosting a dinner in Air Supply's honor, and we were all invited. This was to be a traditional meal, very formal. After a day of sightseeing I got back to the hotel and got ready for our dinner. We all met in the lobby and were taken by car to a restaurant where we would be meeting our hosts.

The restaurant was beautiful and the dinner was set up like a big event. We were all greeted by our hosts and treated like royalty. I learned two things that night; Air Supply is as big as the Beatles in a lot of countries and also countries outside the U.S. consider the crew to be as important as the band. They assume that if you are of a stature worthy of your job you are also important. We were all given a ceremonial key to the city and treated like honored guests.

The dinner consisted of many courses of local and traditional food. There were many toasts made and many honors bestowed on us. That night was one for the books. It has also given me one of my favorite stories to tell. It is the now famous, "Fish Eye Soup" story. I have told this story countless times and it never fails to get a laugh. It is a bit rude, so if you don't care for off color humor, please skip ahead.

One of the courses we were served at this dinner with the Mayor was a traditional soup that consisted of broth, seaweed and fish eyes. This was considered by the locals to be a delicacy. Most of our crew looked at it and turned their noses up. They were not eating this soup. One thing I had always tried on the road was to try local foods, as you never know what you will like, or when you will get the chance again. When you go someplace, anyplace, always assume you may never get there again and do everything you can while there.

Anyway, back to the soup. I tried it, it was all right. I had a few spoonfuls and didn't think anything of it. It was later in the meal that inspiration hit. I took the soup and drank it all without chewing. The rest of the guys looked at me like I was crazy. I think I might have even asked for a second bowl. Wait until tomorrow, I told them. They all thought that tomorrow I would be sick, but I had other plans.

Tomorrow came and I was a little hung over, but not sick. I actually felt pretty good. It was time now to answer natures call and put my plan in action. After using the toilet I quickly called John and told him to come over. When he did I sent him into the bathroom and after a moment he came out laughing hysterically. He had seen what I created. There in the bowl was the brown fish that we all leave behind. Except when John looked at it, it looked back. It had eyes, a lot of them. The mighty brown fish could see

48

for the first time. We called a few of the other guys. Some came, some didn't. But anyone that saw laughed and talked about it for quite a while.

Anyway, you were warned. It isn't pretty, but life on the road isn't all tour buses and catering. The day to day antics are what keep you sane.

The first gig in Taiwan was to take place in an outdoor soccer stadium where they were building us a stage. When we went to the gig to check it out I was surprised at how big the place was, it would hold about thirty thousand people. I thought they have got to be kidding; we'll never fill this place. But we went about the business of setting up our gear anyway. Everything was going fine, sound check went OK and we were show ready. The doors opened and much to my surprise they place was completely filled in a short time. As I said earlier, Air Supply are enormous in a lot of countries. Their music is universal and translates well across borders.

When the lights went down and the band took the stage the roar of the crowd was deafening. The place was absolute mayhem. Once the band started playing the screaming died down and was replaced by thirty thousand voices all singing along. They knew every word, and most of these people did not otherwise speak English. As I said, Air Supply are universal.

Let me be clear about these guys. They are truly rock stars. I have seen them go into countries around the world and rock the house. No big light show, no pyro, no stage set, just their music. They are huge the world over and if they never wrote another song they could still tour the world for the rest of their lives. When I took the gig I was not a fan, but since then and to this day, I am.

Load in at the first gig in Taiwan

An exhausted local crew

We finished the first show and would be heading over to Tainan for the next. It would be another big stadium and another huge crowd. We were able to sightsee a little but a lot of our time was taken up with travel. We drove across Taiwan in a bus to get to our next stop. I got to see a lot of the local countryside from the bus window. This would be the way I would see a lot of countries in the years to come. The second show went well and we would be heading out to The Philippines the next day.

When you are on the road the Tour Manager generally coordinates things like airport runs. He is sort of like the farmer chasing all his chickens and trying to get them together. It is not an easy job. Some of the most talented people in the world can not get the concept of time, schedules, being on time, etc. Our Tour Manager Bernie was an old pro and a great guy. He was in charge and always did a good job. On the departure from Taiwan he had set up cars to get us to the airport and made all the arrangements with the airline. We all convoyed to the airport and Bernie went to the counter to check us in. He got a big surprise, we had missed our flight. He had misread the tickets. This was the first and only time this had happened to him, but this had the potential to be a big problem. He had a party of fifteen people he needed to get to The Philippines for a show. After much scrambling he was able to get us a flight to Hong Kong with a connecting flight to The Philippines the next day. He just had to find hotel rooms for the night, which at the time were scarce.

Before we got on the plane Bernie called the bands travel agent and gave her the task of finding hotel rooms in Hong Kong. He would check in with her once we landed. These were in the days before we all had cell phones. We landed in Hong Kong and Bernie made the call. The travel agent had been able to get one big room, a suite, and apparently we were lucky to get it. Since then I have spent many nights sleeping on an airport floor, so in hindsight I can see we were lucky.

Most of the guys were seasoned pros, so we all made the best of it. This was truly an adventure and made for a really funny night. We got cots and blankets from the hotel, and it was like camp. Fifteen adults all crammed into one suite. You would think there would have been a lot of complaining, but no one did. We were like kids at summer camp. We got through the night and made our flight to The Philippines the next day.

Hong Kong airport

The Philippines

I think that this trip to The Philippines was the first time I saw how hard things can be in other parts of the world. When we landed at the airport in Manila we were met by the local promoter who was waiting with cars to take us to our hotel. In a lot of countries the local promoter or his people will travel with you to make sure all goes well. As it ended up I was one of the last to go, so I went in a car by myself. While we drove to our hotel I saw that there were all sorts of boxes stacked along the road, for miles. I asked my driver what that was all about and he told me that people lived there. These were people with jobs and families and a cardboard box was the best they could do. I was shocked and slowly started to realize how a good portion of the rest of the world lives. I asked the driver to stop so I could talk to some of these people, but I was told it was a bad idea, so we went straight to the hotel. I think they just wanted to get me safely to my room, no need for trouble on the first day.

That image has always stayed with me, those hard working people in the cardboard village. Little hope to improve their lot in life. As I traveled the world I saw more and more of this. I think it is a good idea for everyone to travel outside their home country and see how others live. It will open your eyes and change your life.

Anyway, enough about that, let's get back to Air Supply.

We were staying at the Manila Hotel, a beautiful place. Quite a contrast to the locals I saw on my way in. We were to play two shows at the arena, and they were already sold out. The promoter was asking for a third show, but logistically it would be tough. Other commitments, flights and a host of other reasons would make it hard. But the powers that be would try to work it out. We did the first show and it was another great audience. It was a mirror of the Taiwan crowd. As all went well we headed back to the hotel to crash. Some of the guys were going sightseeing, I wanted to head over to the arena early and make sure all our gear was ok. I have always been more comfortable at the arena on a show day. I think that if I am off relaxing, I won't concentrate on my gig when the time comes. And I truly do love the touring business, so I am always happiest at the gig.

By the morning of the second show it had been worked out that we would stay and perform a third concert. It would be tight, but it would work. So we played the next two shows and went back to the hotel, as we had an early call for our ride to the airport. The next morning started out as uneventful as any. The promoter met us with cars and we loaded our luggage and drove to the airport. When we got there the promoter helped check us in and also informed us that there was a problem. The air controllers had gone on strike, so no planes were flying. With nowhere else to go, we all took our stuff and camped out at the terminal where our plane was. We were told that this happens some times and would be worked out. Well it didn't get worked out, after a while the promoter told us that the military might be on their way to take over the airport. If that happened no planes would fly for a long time, and we would be trapped. Soon after we were told that the military were coming, but there might be a way. Finally we were told that they were flying four or five planes out without air controllers and that if we wanted to see home any time soon we needed to get on the plane and go. With the approaching military and the increasing state of panic at the airport, we did as we were told and hoped for the best. We took off blindly with no air controller and took off; we were the last plane out. And obviously we made it OK, as I am still alive to write these words. It was a little nerve wracking at the time, but still all in a days work.

Once we got in the air and knew we would be all right, there was a sense of relief and excitement. We were going home to the U.S. Not my home, we would be in Los Angeles for a couple of days and I would be heading out to San Pedro to stay with my then girlfriend Teri. This was an exciting time; I had just completed my first international trip and was anxious to see what came next.

These jeep type vehicles were the main source of transportation in Manila. People seemed to just jump on and off randomly, I never saw anyone pay.

Back to the Truck

For the U.S. leg of the tour we would be playing smaller places than we had overseas. We were only carrying band gear, monitors, a monitor desk, a front of house desk and a few lights. With this in mind it had been decided that we would have a small truck for our gear which John and I drove, while the other four crew members would follow by car. The shows were routed so that none of the drives were that long. John and I had managed to negotiate some extra money for truck duty, so I didn't mind.

We would be starting in Grand Rapids, Michigan and we would be leaving from Los Angeles. This meant a couple of days on the road in the truck. We left ourselves plenty of time and had a good road trip out. There's nothing like a good cross country drive when you don't have the pressure of an impossible deadline. I have also had my share of those. You become a connoisseur of truck stops. The greasy food and the crappy souvenir shops sort of draw you in and you start to look forward to them. To this day I enjoy a good truck stop, although I am sad to say that it has been years since I've had the chance to go to one.

We got to Grand Rapids the night before the first show and checked in to the only hotel we could find. As it was winter and freezing out we were disappointed when our rooms had no heat. We were told that the hotel staff was working on it, but it never warmed up. We were happy to check out the next day and head to the gig. Now in the States we weren't carrying a lot of gear, so our load in was not until two or three in the afternoon. As the sound and most of the lights were being provided by the theater each night, this made for an easy day.

The shows in the U.S. went really smooth and the audiences tended to have a lot of regulars. These were people that came to see the band every year, and who would stop by the hotel bar after the show. A lot of them had become friends with the band over the years. When the show was over the load out literally took less than an hour. The band would stay in the city we played that night, but the crew would drive to the next city and get a hotel. Doing this left us time to deal with any travel emergencies that might come up, like a breakdown.

It wasn't long before we developed a system for after show travel. We would load out, fast, and while the band were doing their meet and greet, we would go to their dressing room and steal all their beer and food. I don't think they realized it was us taking their stuff until late in the tour. They had assumed that the building staff had just cleaned up early. When we told them they laughed and thought that was pretty good. As I said, these guys were old pros who had seen it all.

We would eat in the truck and whoever wasn't driving would drink all the beer. On many a night I was on the running board of the truck doing sixty miles an hour, relieving myself. When you drink that much beer if you stop every time you have to go you would never get anywhere. The rest of the crew would be behind us in a car taking bets on how long it would be before I fell off. I never did. But I did lob a lot of empty beer cans at their car.

The relaxed atmosphere of the gigs and late load in times made for a tour that was more like a vacation than work. We worked our way across the northeast and down the east coast. We did two nights at Westbury Music Fair which was the gig closest to home for me. It was cool because I had family members who were fans that not only got to see the show, but they got to meet the guys, which was cool. The last shows on this leg were in Florida, where we had a few days off. It was nice to be warm; we had been doing shows up north in the cold, so a day off by the pool was just what the doctor ordered. We finished up our shows and got ready to do the next and last leg of the tour, South America.

View from the truck window

South America

South America back in the eighties was a wild place.
There is a lot I would like to talk about, but I don't
think this book is the right place. Just use your
imagination; it was all that and more.

Our promoter rep from South America met us at our
last U.S. gig and would stay with us and make sure
we got safely to our shows. Manny was a fun guy
who knew the ropes down there, so it was a good idea
to have him along. He flew over with us and when we
got to Columbia we were met by his associates with
ground transportation. Air Supply was also huge
down there so security was a big concern. We were
taken from the airport by car to a private disco they
had rented out for our dinner and a party. When we
got there we were provided with   and   and
also   and some local   . Fill in the blanks, you
will probably be right. Oh and the food was good too.

The shows were great, stadium sized again. Our
nights off were another culture shock for me. The
local promoters had private tables for us at just about
every club there was. The promoter reps would ask
me where I wanted to go, and wherever we went there
was already a table reserved for Air Supply. I don't
think I paid for a drink or anything else the whole
trip. It did make me uneasy that we always had armed
guards with us, but you get used to it. South America,
namely Columbia has some beautiful scenery. After
our shows in Columbia we had one last big party
before we parted ways. The party went until dawn
and I ended up riding on the back of a flatbed truck
all the way to the airport. I was going home.

Rules of the road:

Own a secure locking suitcase

At the hotel always lock up your valuables in the suitcase

Don't have guests spend the night

If you have an overnight guest, don't fall asleep until she leaves

If you aren't sure you'll stay awake, set the alarm and be up first

Never ever have a mini bar key

Falling asleep with a new friend in the room can result in the loss of all your valuables, and an empty mini bar which can cost between $150 - $250

Everything

There was a difference between the time I came home from the Gibson tour, and when I was done with Air Supply. This time I knew what my next job was. Almost since the moment I met him, Steve Botting and I became the best of friends. He was the Production Manager / Sound Engineer for The Bangles and he had asked me long ago if I would be interested in doing their next tour, which was in a couple of months. I would have about two months off before rehearsals started, which was great. I had some money in the bank and could always find work to tide me over. This was one of the only times I took a temp job, since I knew exactly when my next gig was, and didn't need to look for a tour.

I took a job at a company called Panafax, which was a fax machine company. I worked in the warehouse stocking product, driving a forklift, etc. The work was easy and the hours were regular, so I just auto piloted it there for a while. One problem you have when you are in the position I was in, you can't tell people what your normal job is, they won't believe you. People have this pre conceived notion that anyone that tours for a living would never be anywhere normal. More than once I had seen friends try to tell someone what they did for a living and most were called liars right to their face. I always had a cover story; I would tell people I was a landscaper. At Panafax when they offered me a full time job that's what I told them, thanks but no thanks. When it came time to leave I just told them that landscaping was starting to pick up, and I had to go.

Anyway, back to The Bangles. The new CD was called "Everything" and John and I would be doing our third tour together on this one. I was going to take care of bass and keyboards, and John would work for the two guitar players. One of Steve's friends, Nick would be the drum tech. Rehearsals were in L.A. and the tour would head out on the theater / college circuit.

The rehearsals went for a couple of weeks and we did full production rehearsals with stage set, sound and lights. This was a bigger show than the band had put on before so everything had to be perfect. Everything went well and the band got to know us a little bit while working together. It is always hard at the beginning, a band doesn't know you or what to expect. There is always a lot riding on getting the show off without a problem and the band has to put their full faith in you and hope for the best. Without Steve's endorsement I don't think they would have been able to get comfortable with us quickly enough. With rehearsals behind us we were ready to head out and start the tour.

As I said we would be playing small theaters and colleges. The theater shows were always interesting as a lot of the old theaters have a lot of history dating back to the vaudeville days. I'm a big fan of vaudeville, so it was great to roam the old theaters. Sometimes there would be a stagehand that had worked at the theater long enough to know some of the theaters old stories, and would also know where all the old nooks and crannies were. These gigs were great for that reason, but most of the old theaters were hard to load into, as they were not built for rock and roll. A lot would be on busy main thoroughfares and some had no way to get the truck close so you had to dump your gear in the street and push. I remember one gig where the load in door was one story above the stage and they used a ramp with a rope and pulley to get the gear to stage level. I have even seen cranes used to haul the gear up to the load in. As I said, I love the history, but not the load in or lack of stage room to work.

The colleges we played were a different story. Most of the halls had more than enough room so you could dump all the trucks at once. This was especially good in the colder climates as the instruments needed to acclimate to the room. On the college circuit a lot of times for lunch they would have a big barbeque set up where someone from catering would cook. My favorite gigs were the ones where they let me man the grill. I did this whenever I could. I guess it was a little taste of home after being away for a while, a little bit of normalcy.

One gig on this tour that stands out was when we played the Naval Academy at Annapolis. We had a stage set up in the hall where we would be playing, but the day of the show there was also a boxing tournament set up at the far end. All our stagehands were cadets at the academy and they were some of the best stagehands I have ever seen. They didn't care that we were a long haired rock and roll crew; they addressed us as sir, and did exactly what we asked them to do. The only deviation was when their school won over at the boxing ring, these guys would go crazy for a minute and then right back to work. Easily some of the best local crew I ever worked with.

When show time came everything started off as planned. There were a few points in the show where both guitar players needed to do a guitar change at the same time. At these times I would go over to John's side of the stage and take one guitar and do one of the changes. The first time I did this you could hear a few cadets in the front row start to chant "Elvis, Elvis". Each time I would go out on stage to work there were a few more people yelling. I started to notice that the guitar player Susannah wasn't coming over to the edge of the stage as much. She was staying right out on stage so I would have to go to her. This of course would get the Elvis chant going, which by now everyone was laughing about. Toward the end of the show a microphone stand mysteriously fell over center stage and I had to go out and stand it up. Of course when I did, the lighting guy had the spotlight operators put their lights on me and the crowd was joined by our sound guy Steve, with a microphone through the sound system, yelling Elvis. It got really loud with the whole audience yelling. That was just one of those moments you could never plan, but we still talk about. I'll give you one guess what my nickname was for the rest of the tour.

Later on the tour we had a day off in Memphis and the band went to Graceland. After that, during interviews when they were asked about their song "Eternal Flame" which was on the charts at the time, they would segue from that to the eternal flame at Graceland, to the Elvis story I have just told you. After that tour even some of my friends at home called me Elvis. I guess the King does live on.

Platinum

When the Bangles tour was almost over, Steve our Production Manager told the crew that as a thank you, the band would be giving each of us a platinum album award. In the music business this is the brass ring, the best that you could do. I was really impressed, I was in my early twenties and was about to receive my first platinum record. I was anxious to get it; this was a sort of validation for my career. A lot of my family still thought that I had a hokey fly by night job with no future.

We were told that the awards would be shipped to each of us at our homes. I couldn't wait, I was so nervous that mine would get lost or damaged. Every day I would wait for the mailman and accost him on the front lawn. Every day I was skunked, he didn't have it. After the mailman I would wait for any sign of the UPS man, in case he had it. I didn't know how the record was going to be shipped, so I had to keep my eyes open.

One day I came home to find a box at my front door, about the right size and shape, it had been left outside unprotected! I grabbed it and quickly went inside, my hands shaking as I started to open it. When I got it open I thought for a moment that I heard the angels sing. There it was in all its platinum glory, with my name engraved right on it. I stared at it a lot that day. I had to keep looking at it to make sure my name was still on it.

Electric

The Bangles tour was finishing up just as Debbie Gibson was starting rehearsals for her next tour. As the years went by I was lucky enough that this became a pattern, jump from one tour to the next. At one point I had to get a second workbox made so I could have my tools shipped out in time for my next tour, while I finished up the tour I was on.

Debbie's next tour would be called "Electric Youth" after her new album that had already gotten singles on the charts. This was going to be a bigger show with a larger stage set. We would also be playing much bigger buildings, mostly arenas. The tour production rehearsals would be taking place at our local arena.

John Karlquist and I would be on this one together again. When we finished The Bangles tour Debbie and the band had already been rehearsing in the studio she had built in the basement of the new house. There were some new faces and some old faces in the band, along with a new tech, a keyboard guy who had been at the rehearsals while John and I were away.

I would be working for a new drummer, Fred Levine, and Adam the percussionist/ sax player from the last tour. One of the new musicians was Gary Corbett on keyboards. I immediately recognized him, he was in Paul Stanley's band on his solo club tour, I had stage managed a show at a local rock club called Showcase. Gary was a regular rock and roll guy like me and felt equally out of place. We became good friends on that tour, and ended up touring together and doing local shows for years.

As rehearsals had already been under way for a while there wasn't too much for me to do except make sure everyone's gear was road ready, and that we had all the supplies we needed. I had to make sure everyone had proper road cases so that their gear would survive being on the trucks for the tour. Also when you start out a tour like this you need to make a manifest of all your gear. That includes all manufacture info, serial numbers, value etc. It is easier to do this in rehearsals so you can take your time and get it right. A manifest is used when you tour outside the country so that customs knows what was yours. This is also important for insurance purposes, in case anything happens during shipping.

Working on a manifest during rehearsals is also good busy work, so that if a band guy tries to get you to get them a cup of coffee, soda, lunch, or anything, you can tell them you're too busy and to get it themselves. This can be an important step at the beginning of a tour. You set the tone that you are not a gopher; you are a pro at what you do and are not subservient. Don't get me wrong, on a show day whatever they need or want on that stage to do a show, it's my job to make sure they have it, but at other times they need to know that I am not their personal assistant. Most band guys are cool, and I normally don't mind making a coffee run, but I have had a few that thought it was part of my job to carry their luggage or wash their chain mail shirts, it isn't.

Off track again, I am easily distracted when giving opinions, let's get back to our story so far. The Electric Youth Tour, a big production with a large staff that sold out almost anywhere we went. We had moving lights, moving set pieces, and a piano that rose out of the floor. Singers, dancers, costume changes. Debbie is a very talented performer and this tour really showcased her talents.

Production rehearsals were at the Nassau Coliseum, our local arena. It had been rented out by the production so that we could set up all the gear and work out any potential problems. It was good to rehearse with all the show elements, it gave everyone involved time to make sure they had what they needed to do their job. It was cool working in the Coliseum; it was where I had always gone to see concerts as a kid. Production rehearsals can have long days for the crew. Typically we would all get there early in the morning and work on equipment or programming. The band would usually get there about four, and then we would run through the show for as long as it took to get things right.

There really wasn't any excitement or any good stories during this time. We all worked and did our jobs, and got to know our fellow crew guys a little. We loaded out and headed over to our first stop so we could start this tour. I was looking forward to this one, as usual. I would be going to England, Australia and Japan for the first time. It seemed like each tour I was covering a little more ground, which was great.

And also on this tour, as on the first, we would be shooting a full length concert video. It is always cool when a tour does that. So many of these shows come and go, it's nice to have a copy of a show you worked on. Also on this tour we did the "Arsenio Hall" show. He used to shoot on the Paramount lot, which was cool for me as I am a Star Trek fan, and that is where "Star Trek" is shot. I never was able to get on their set, but it was still cool being there. It was great doing the Arsenio show and then watching it that night. At this point working on television was still new to me. It was on that show I first worked with Johnny Caswell, another great guy. Throughout my career I did many award shows with him, he always took care of the band instruments for all the big shows, and he would always go out of his way to help you.

Less than a month into the U.S. tour we went over to England to open for a group named "Bros." at Wembley Stadium. The group was comprised of two twin brothers, Matt and Luke Goss, and their band. These guys were huge over there; this was a good chance for Debbie to play in front of a lot of people in England. We had a lot of time off, and the sightseeing was great. The show went over well and as it turned out, Bros. would be coming to the states to open for Debbie. They hadn't really cracked the American market, so this was a good opportunity for them. They were cool guys and having them out on tour turned out OK.

The rest of the U.S. leg of the tour went fine, we only had a couple of incidents that we could have done without. Both happened at the hometown shows in New York, one at the Coliseum and one at Madison Square Garden. I can't remember which happened where, I will just tell the stories.

At one point Debbie would rise out of the floor playing her piano. This was a high point in the show and on one night in particular as she was rising through the floor the piano didn't work. You couldn't hear anything coming out of it. Eventually one of the keyboard players started playing the parts. There was an electronic problem that was not foreseen. She carried on like a pro, but you couldn't help but feel bad for her.

The other problem was when something became jammed in the lift that brought up the piano and it wouldn't go back down after the song. It was right in the way of all the dancers and performers. One by one the crew all tried to get it to go. You could hear us whacking it with hammers. Finally it went and the problem was corrected before the next show. But again, these two Spinal Tap moments had to happen at the hometown shows.

Later during the U.S. tour we went over to Japan. Japan is every crew guys dream, the people are great, and the country is beautiful. The entire culture is based on doing their best to help you. Every tour I have ever done there has been handled by Udo Artists. Mr. Udo is the biggest promoter there and his people are all first rate.

When you do shows in Japan the show times are early compared to what we are used to. A show may start at six or seven and there is no opening act. That means that you can be done for the night and heading for the hotel by eight or nine. And the crews there are truly amazing. Given the opportunity they will have as much of your gear set up as you let them. They will take pictures of the gear and make notes so that everything is perfect when you get there. They are nothing short of amazing. Mr. Udo and his people make it a pleasure to tour Japan.

Most of the times there we would stay in the same hotel and bullet train to the different gigs. There were always people from Udo Artists with us to make sure everything went perfectly. They would also organize things for us to do on days off. If there was something in particular you wanted to do or see, they would do their best to make it happen. And every time I have been to Japan, Mr. Udo and his people have always taken the band and crew out for a Kobe Beef dinner. This is one of the best dinners you can have in Japan, and it was always in one of the best restaurants around. Mr. Udo always made sure it was a special night.

There was one mishap on this trip that I just remembered. Sometimes I can act without thinking which never really ends well. One night at the hotel, after a few drinks, I was hanging out with the bass player and we decided it would be really cool to trash Fred the drummers' room. We weren't sure how, but we were on a mission. We headed upstairs to his floor and did our version of a recon mission. We saw that the coast was clear but there was no way we could get into his room, we tried everything. As we all know, once started, the mission has to be completed. We noticed a fire extinguisher just down the hall, and that seemed perfect. One of us (it doesn't matter who) grabbed the fire extinguisher, aimed the hose under the door, and let fly with a ten second burst. Neither of us realized that it was one that shoots a fine powder everywhere.

The Aftermath:

Fred was not happy. He called the Tour Manager and got a new room. Everything he owned had to be dry-cleaned. His old room would take two days to clean and someone had to pay the rental on the room and for the cleaning. The police were called. It is only by the grace of God and a fast talking Tour Manager that our entire party was not thrown out of the hotel in the middle of the night. After all this happened the Tour Manager went down his list of suspects, and I was at the top of that list. I owned up and eventually so did my partner in crime. Aside from the yelling at I got, I fully expected to get fired, but I didn't.

The Aftermath Part 2:

The damage to the room came to just over eight hundred dollars, so my half was just over four hundred dollars. The dry cleaning wasn't cheap, so all told I think I paid about five hundred and fifty dollars. At this point I just wanted to pay and put it behind me. I still had to deal with my Production Manager, Omar, and tell him. He also could fire me for this. At the next gig I went into his office, told him what happened, and told him that if I was getting fired it was cool, I deserved it. I did not expect the reaction I got. He was barely able to contain his laughter. It was still a big deal, just a funny one that wasn't getting me fired.

The Aftermath Part 3:

I also was surprised at the reaction my crew mates had to this whole affair. I expected to be berated, but they all loved it. Each guy on the crew chipped in to cover my end of the damages. They were essentially buying a part of my crime because they all wished they had done it. In the end I think I was out about thirty dollars. And Fred appreciated the joke, since all had been paid for. All in all I was a lot better off than

I thought I would be. And by the way, it was me that fired off the fire extinguisher.

Before I conclude my Japan story, I have to mention George Silk. Our first morning in Tokyo, John and I decided to leave the hotel, walk around the city and get breakfast. We weren't far from the hotel when a man came chasing after us. When he caught up to us he introduced himself as George Silk. I don't know what his real name was, he went by a name that was easy for us to pronounce. He told us that he had the best souvenir shop in town, and that we should come over later for a barbeque. He could tell when he saw us that we were in town with a tour, and he wanted the whole crew to come by. His shop was on an incredibly busy street right in the middle of Tokyo, and he had a little patch of grass where he would barbeque.

That was his sales technique, inviting you over for beer and barbeque, and he was brilliant at it. He never asked me to buy anything, but the entire crew ended up at his place drinking, eating and buying. It got to be a joke with my crewmates, they would go out in the morning and when they passed Georges place I would already be there, fixing chairs for the next barbeque, hanging flags, having a beer. George was a truly interesting person and by the end of the trip, he had been deemed by my crew as my official Japanese dad. Every trip to Japan I talk about in this book will have stories about George.

George Silk at his shop

Sight seeing in Japan one beer at a time

Australia

After Japan it was time to go back to the U.S. to finish that leg of the tour, before going to Australia. The rest of the U.S. shows went well and it wasn't long before we were on a plane for some long flights down under.

Australia is a beautiful country. The flight there was around twenty something hours, but it felt like three days. When I asked my production manager Omar how long the flight was he gave me another nugget of his wisdom. He told me "Get on the plane and start drinking, get drunk and pass out. When you wake up, start drinking until you get drunk and pass out again, when you wake up the second time we'll be there." As it turned out, he was right, that was how far it was, I checked. We got to Australia, got to the hotel, met with the promoter and got started.

The shows all went fine; there really weren't any stories to tell here either. This crew had been working together for a long time at this point and I think we were all ready for a break. After the last show the whole production went out for one last party, which for some of us went on longer than for others. With the help of a local lighting guy named Motley that I had made friends with, I did not miss my flight home. He and I were on the same first morning flight, and when I didn't show at the lobby he broke into my room, kicked me out of bed, tossed my stuff in my suitcase and got both of us to the airport. Motley, I still owe you one.

By now I was anxious to get home for a little time off. While I was on this tour my friend Al Pitrelli had gotten the gig of guitar player / music director with Alice Cooper. He had asked me to guitar / keyboard tech for the rehearsals and tour, but I was already committed to the Gibsons. We had reached and arrangement though, I would miss rehearsals and the first run through Europe and pick up the tour in Canada right after Christmas. I was glad it worked out, Al and I had worked the clubs together for years, so this was a big step up for both of us. Also I had been an Alice Cooper fan since I was a kid, so I was really looking forward to this one.

The Sydney Opera House

My first Kangaroo

Rules of the road:

Never leave your guest on the bus unescorted

Never leave the bus unlocked

Never use the bus toilet for #2

Never lend out your bus key

Never leave any valuables on the bus, or in your bunk

Don't leave your crap all over the bus, other people live there

If you are right handed, take a bunk on the drivers' side

If you are left handed, take a bunk on the passenger side

The bus driver will clean the bus, but respect him and his bus. Pick up after yourself

Trash

Alice's new record was called "Trash" and there was a serious buzz in the industry about it. A lot of work had been put into it with an assortment of big names in the music business. This record was looking to be a big success for Alice. It is amazing to see how many successful musicians (I hate the term rock star), looked up to Alice and site him as a major influence. There are a lot of bands out there that would not have existed if not for the Coop.

I flew into Canada the day before the first show, and most of my new crew mates were already stationed at the hotel bar. My friend Nick Morley from the Bangles tour was the drum tech. He introduced me to the other guitar tech, Kevin "Batty" Walsh. I also met the stage manager, Tom "Putter T" Hanlon who seemed like a cool guy. A lot of these crew guys had been with the Coop for a number of years. As I was to find out, the Cooper organization was a very loyal one. If you did your job without a problem you were the first phone call for the next tour.

Alice had been with his manager Shep since day one, and Toby, one of the other management team, had also been around forever. Alice had an assistant named Brian Nelson who had been with him a number of years as well. These guys are all still there. In fact, not too long ago I went to an Alice show and when I saw Brian in catering he said "Welcome home". It struck me then why I had stayed with the Coop all the years I did, it was home. The fact that Brian said that meant he understood it too. The Cooper organization is comprised of a number of diverse people with a lot of different backgrounds, but somehow it does become a family. Changes in my life had caused me to get a job that kept me home; otherwise I would still be out there with the Coop.

There I go again, off point, let's get back to the Trash tour. When I started with the Coop in December, in Canada, they were having a record cold winter up there. Nothing was warm. On the bus we slept in our coats, and the gigs never seemed to warm up at all. It didn't help that a lot of the gigs were hockey arenas with plywood down over the ice.

Alice's band members were all guys about my age so there was a lot of common ground. This tour the crew and band actually hung out a lot, even on days off. Besides Al, Derek Sherinian the keyboard player was the other guy I worked for. Both Al and Derek had big rigs so I had a lot to do. Stage right was comprised of Tommy "T-Bone" Carradonna on bass, and Pete Freezin' on guitar. On drums there was Jonathan Mover, and somewhere in there was a background singer.

The shows were really high energy aside from also being very theatrical. The floor was a reflective mylar that the lighting guys used to bounce light effects around the arena. There were set pieces all over the stage that looked like giant spikes, but would turn around and on the other side were just full of body parts. Center stage there was a giant trash can that at one point, Freddy Kruger would pop out of and attack Alice. And of course, there was the guillotine. There was even a video segment at the beginning of the nightmare section of the show. There were so many other elements to the stage I could spend pages describing them. Let's just say that it was a show to see. On this leg the opening act was a band called Great White, who were always a great live act to see.

The Canadian tour was a good introduction to the tour. The shows were all pretty good sized venues, so the entire show could be set up without changing things too much. There was one show where the snow storm was so bad that we didn't get to the arena until late in the afternoon. We all pitched in and got the show up and did the gig. Actually, in all my years with Alice, I can't recall a gig ever being cancelled. On the way to this particular gig, the merchandise truck slid off the road and pretty far down a hill. The merchandise people still made it to the gig. We were all impressed.

After the Canadian tour two things happened, we found out that we would be going to Los Angeles to do The American Music Awards, and that Jonathan Mover was leaving the band. So there would be some auditions while in L.A. It's always sad to see someone leave early, but it happens. I would be going to L.A. for the show and auditions, which was fine by me, I love it out there.

The auditions were set up so that we could get them done right away, there was still a lot of tour booked and whoever got the gig would need to learn the songs. There would be only three guys auditioning, Jimmy DeGrasso, who had played with Al in Talas, Eric Singer, and a friend of someone else's, I think his name was Chuck, but don't quote me. As Jimmy was from out of town I let him stay with me at my place, I had plenty of room and had known him a while. Karma must have been on my side that day because when Jimmy was staying with me he introduced me to one of my favorite places in the world, Barnies Beanery. It was a roadhouse style place that had been around forever, and I have never been more at home anywhere. They have the best burgers and beer period. For the rest of my life I will owe Jimmy for taking me there. I still go whenever I can.

Back to the auditions, everyone played great but we all know who got the gig. Eric Singer is still with Alice all these years later. I guess he was a good fit. It was cool because Eric's tech Ralph was someone that I grew up with. The production people weren't sure about hiring the new drummers' tech, but when I told Dan and Putter that he was cool, he was in. That's how it works, it's all about knowing someone on the inside that will vouch for you .And thank God Ralph got the gig, he has provided us with more great stories than you can ever imagine. He is a very animated guy with a heart of gold. I said it before; you will see many of his stories in this book.

We did the American Music Awards, which went OK. At this point doing television was becoming commonplace for me; it was actually cool to do the award shows. I spent a little time in L.A. before heading home. I knew there would be rehearsals before the U.S. leg of the tour, so a little down time was a good thing.

Stage Diving

Let me share a few words regarding stage diving. I'm
sure we have all been to a show or heard about a
show where a member of the audience ran onto the
stage, and how they were quickly ushered off. I have
heard complaints from a lot of people wondering why
it's such a big deal, if the fan wants to be there with
the performer why does the crew run to grab them so
fast. There are actually a lot of good reasons for this.

I have seen people run on stage and trip over gear,
getting hurt while also breaking a piece of show vital
equipment. You have to remember, it is the crews job
to get the show on with no problems. If someone
came running through your work space damaging
things, you might take issue. The second reason is
that when people rush onstage, they are usually
pumped with adrenaline, running full bore toward a
band member. In the rush of excitement, they usually
don't realize how fast they are going, and they can
run into the musician so hard that they knock them
down, causing injury. You also have to remember,
this show is the crews' livelihood and an injured
musician can cause shows to be cancelled and put
people out of work.

Now let me give some advice to any potential stage
jumpers. If you find yourself onstage at a concert and
a crew guy comes toward you to get you off stage, go
quietly with him, you are done. Or stage dive back
into the audience. You may feel that it is your right to
be on stage, that you earned it, but you don't belong
there. If you resist when someone tries to get you
offstage, they will use force to get you out of there. If
you are feeling tough and think you can take on the

dumb roadie, remember this, that roadie is faster and stronger than he looks, he does this every day. Something else to remember, if you take on that roadie and somehow win, the entire stage area, on all sides and back, are filled with other roadies that will come out and kick your ass, hard.

I have seen it too many times, if I was grabbing someone and another kid got by me. Not only will they get their ass kicked, at the very least they will get thrown out of the arena, and at worst they might get carted off to jail. Remember, if on stage; go along quietly with the nice roadie.

And a quick note about throwing things on stage, don't. You can still injure your favorite rock star and end the show early. And never throw anything dangerous. With increased security at venues that isn't the problem it used to be. Back in the day I've seen steel darts and knives whizz by me and stick in a wall near where I was working. That and explosives like m-80s, just don't do it. If you are spotted, a lot of the crew will come after you, and there will be a bad ass kicking before you go to jail.

Because a show is something that people pay to see, and get excited about, they forget that those people working on stage are just doing their jobs. Show them the same respect that you would expect in your cubicle at work.

Trash in the U.S.

The next leg of the tour was going to be in the States, playing large theaters, outdoor amphitheaters called sheds, and some larger buildings. One of the support acts was a band called Danger Danger, who I had worked for back in the clubs. Also, Alice's guitar player Al Pitrelli had been a member of the band when they first formed. Their crew consisted of my friends Todd and Howie, and a soundman named Carl I had also known from the clubs back home. Between them, our newly acquired drum tech Ralph, and Al we had what was deemed the "Long Island Mafia" on the road. This was a really cool time for all of us. We had all knocked around the clubs together for years, and now we were all on a successful tour together. At one point even Charlie Milton came out on the Danger Danger crew.

So now we were on a tour where the band and crew all hung out, and the crew from the support act was also like family. The tour had been great up until now, but at this point it was just fun all the time. Days off were a blast, we would all manage to hook up and find some trouble and get into it. It got to a point where the days off were more tiring than gig days. There was even a time where I turned off all the lights in my hotel room and didn't answer the phone, just so I could catch up on my rest.

Bigga Gigs

Up until now I have been hinting about the Ralph stories that will appear on these pages. It is at this point that most of them originate. Again I would like to be clear, when I tell these stories I am in no way making fun of Ralph. He has been a friend of mine for what seems like forever, and he has a good heart. He also just happens to be very colorful when he expresses himself. Having him on tour would lighten the mood on even the toughest day.

One day on tour there were a few of us hanging out in the dressing room just killing time. One of the band guys asked if there was a tuning room at the gig. Now a tuning room would traditionally be a place where the musicians could tune up and warm up in a quiet environment. We never really had a tuning room because the crew tuned the instruments and we used electronic tuners, so noise in the arena would not be a problem.

It was at this time that Ralph generated what has become a classic line. I will include his hand gestures as they were an integral part .He said " I thought at the Bigga Gigs (arm raised in front of you, hand going up and down) the tuning room was automatic" (arm waist high, hand flat , bring hand and arm left to right). This immediately put everyone in the room on the floor with laughter. The term "Bigga Gigs" and the term "Automatic" have been used and reused and have become legend. To this day if you even do the slightest part of the hand gesture, people will know exactly what you mean.

The Chicago Story

The tour through the States went pretty much the same. Gig days were a blast, working with the Long Island mafia. The days off were usually spent first at the mall, then a good restaurant, and then a bar somewhere. We never ended up back at the hotel early; it was usually way past closing time. One night in Chicago was an exceptional night. We had already been to a couple of bars and were pretty hammered. We flagged a cab in our drunken stupor and told him to take us to Johnny Rockets. He tried to tell us we didn't need a cab, but we weren't having it. We demanded in no uncertain terms that he take us there. I think we may even have insulted his family and suggested that his father could have been a farm animal. Anyway, we closed the door on the cab, he pulled a u turn and there we were, Johnny Rockets. It was across the street from where we grabbed the cab. He charged us twenty bucks, cursed us, and sped off. I can't say I blame him.

This was one of those nights where we all kind of split off later in the evening. I ended up back in my hotel room, which had an adjoining door to Ralph's room. Sometime that night I decided I needed to get my stuff packed to make the morning easier. As Ralph had borrowed my radio, and wasn't home yet, I did what any drunken idiot would do, I kicked down the adjoining door and got my radio. The next morning I realized my mistake and called the front desk. I asked, "How much is a door?" I thought they might have kept a price sheet around for such eventualities, to which they replied "why". I tried to explain to them that the door was kicked in and I needed to pay for it. They told me that they had no report of a broken door, to which I tried to tell them, of course there is no report, I just kicked it in. They ended up sending security and maintenance to my room to check this out. I opened the adjoining door and showed them the broken debris in Ralph's room, with Ralph still passed out in his bed. When they stepped through to survey the damage I closed my door and left them in the other room with Ralph. He woke up to a room full of strange men with tools and reports. He was not happy. There was talk of arrest, there were threats made but in the end, the damage was paid for and after all, we did have a lot of rooms booked. By the way, at that time a door went for two hundred dollars.

Our Tour Manager Vince saw the hotel security log for the night and asked for a copy. All our crimes were in there. Apparently Batty had broken into the kitchen during the night to make a cheese and onion sandwich. Security was none too pleased that a half naked guy was in the kitchen brandishing a butter knife making some food. Anyway Vince had gotten the security report to show the Coop, I guess to get us in trouble. The band guys told me that the Coop just laughed about it. You see, no one was hurt and all damages were paid for. The Coop understood what it was like to be young and on the road. He had been there himself.

Another Night Off

At this stage in the game I have to be honest, I was drinking fairly heavily, most of us were. But I would tend to go a little too far. By this time I would drink Everclear, which is pure grain alcohol, if it was available. This is not a smart thing to do. Drinking Everclear straight can kill you, its one hundred and ninety proof. But I drank it anyway. I only tell you this because it's a part of my next story.

I was out one night with Ralph and a guy named John from the lighting crew. We were in a local bar out in the middle of nowhere. Now when a group of guys with long hair and leather jackets from out of town go into a local bar, we would usually be viewed as unwelcome strangers. The locals just didn't get us, and it wasn't unusual for some of the local idiots to try and show how tough they were by harassing the long haired rock and roll guys. You could usually tell when you first walked into a place if it was a bad idea. My radar must have been set off because for some reason I decided to hang back a little, which was not my norm. Normally if something stupid needed to be done I was the volunteer, but not this night.

We started out in a booth, but eventually John and Ralph ended up talking to people at different ends of the bar. I think Ralph actually new someone there, and John was making a mess out of hitting on a local girl. I was hanging back at the booth drinking shots of Everclear and chasing them with beer. After a while you could almost see it coming, John was creating a lot of tension with the girl he was hitting on and her friends. And I could hear things starting to get a little loud where Ralph was at the bar; some sort of a ruckus was brewing.

When you've seen things go bad before, you can tell when things are about to go bad again. I had been in enough bars where I had worn out my welcome that I could tell these guys had just about worn ours out. Now I'm not one to be easily chased off or run from a fight, but at this point in my life I was done trying to take on all the locals. When you know you're gonna get your ass kicked, it's time for a new plan.

I heard some sort of a loud yell come from the bar, and my survival instinct must have kicked in. Without even thinking I poured my shot of Everclear on the booth table and dropped a lit match. That stuff is more flammable than gasoline .As soon as the table caught fire I was on my feet and headed for the door. I hit the door running and didn't look back for three blocks. Fortunately, Ralph and John had done the math; they saw the fire and me heading out the door and knew it was time to go. When I finally turned around they were about a half a block behind me. We stopped to catch our breath and realized no one was in pursuit.

As we were walking back to our hotel laughing about what just happened, you would think we would have had enough sense to just go home. But no, we ended up in another local bar and wore out our welcome there also; only this place didn't serve Everclear.

Ralph and the Chicken Wings

I have been told that once I start on Ralph stories I tend to go on for a while. I guess that is true. Here goes another one. We were at a gig in the mid-west somewhere and an old friend of Ralph's showed up. He owned a club in town and Ralph had been through there many times on tour. After the show they wanted to hook up for a few drinks and catch up, so Ralph asked us if we would cover him for load out. This is fairly common; we would always help each other out. So we loaded out the gear while Ralph went with his buddy.

Most nights on tour the after show food is pretty good. The promoter will load a hot meal on the bus for when the crew was done working. Sometimes the food is a local specialty, like cheese steaks when you play Philadelphia. Sometimes it's just pizza, which is OK too. Sometimes it's not so great and you just deal with it. This particular night we had one hundred chicken wings for ten guys, pretty lame. No big deal, you just make do.

Ralph had finished hanging out with his buddy while we were still in the venue, and he had gone straight to the bus. When Batty and I got there we found him with a little buzz on, sitting in the booth of the front lounge surrounded by chicken bones. He had already eaten over half the wings that were meant for a crew of ten. We immediately jumped right on him for eating everyone else's wings, which to our surprise, he denied. There he was, the only one on the bus, surrounded by bones, with at least ten wings worth of chicken still stuck in his teeth, swearing he didn't do it. We hammered him and hammered him about it, but he would not budge. He swore it was not him. When the rest of the crew arrived everyone each took a turn accusing him, and still he didn't budge. It wasn't him; it was some mysterious chicken wing thief. In truth, the eating of the food wasn't a big deal. It was the disregard for the other guys on the crew that created the offense. On the road you have to get each others back, and the chicken wing incident was more of a breach of the code of the road. Ralph continued stonewalling for days and when he finally admitted that he ate the wings, he said that it was the fear of what we would do to him that made him deny his crime.

You see another facet of life on the road is the boredom you deal with. The bus rides are long and the days off can sometimes be repetitive. So we never really miss out on a chance to harass a fellow crew member. It's all in good fun, just not a lot of fun when you're on the receiving end. We gave Ralph grief for weeks over the wings. And now, years later, I will probably get a ton of grief from Ralph for including this story. But it's a price I'm willing to pay.

Rules of the road:

Bus food is there for everyone working

Bus food is not for your guests

Make sure there is enough food for the whole crew

First guy on the bus, ice down the beer

Leave some food for the driver

First guy on the bus, stock the back lounge cooler

Never pull apart three good sandwiches to make yourself a really great one

And finally, never leave Ralph alone with the chicken wings

Australian Folklore

At the end of the U.S. leg we were heading down to Australia where Alice was really popular. One of our crew (names aren't important), was regaling the band with his stories of Australia. You see, he has been there once, for three days, and stayed on a farm and played one gig. He was an obvious expert on all things Australian. He was sitting with the band guys, most of which or all had not been to Australia, telling them what it would be like.

"Wait till we get to Australia" he said, "we're all gonna get laid," "There's four women for every man there, da men, dey never rejuvenated after da war" he told them. "Heh, heh, heh" was his sinister laugh as he shared this information.

I still haven't figured out what war, or why the men needed to rejuvenate. I did realize at the time that some new catch phrases were being sent my way, and I had better make a note.

Again, though, this was a long flight, and they are hard to get used to. I don't remember how many hours we were in the air, but it seemed like forever. I was looking forward to this trip, as usual. Alice was booked all over Australia, with some multiple night gigs. There were a lot of days off, and since I had been here six months ago, I knew a lot of cool local stuff to do. The guys and I were going to check out animal sanctuaries and see kangaroos among other things. With the family like atmosphere that the band and crew had, this stop was a lot like a vacation.

Trash in Australia

We landed in Sydney, where we had a day off. It's a great city to spend time in. Between the Opera House, Bondi Beach, Tooronga Park Zoo, and The Rocks, this is what they call their area with a lot of pubs, one of the best pub crawls around. There was something for everyone to do. Usually I will try to do it all.

I struck out on my own for a bit, a lot of the guys wanted to crash after the flight. But we all did make a plan to go to Tooronga and see some kangaroos and other local animals. It was a short ferry ride across the harbor. It's a great wildlife sanctuary with amazing facilities for the animals.

The shows were all in good size buildings and as I said we had multiple nights in Melbourne and Sydney. We were able to see a lot of the country and this leg of the tour also had a stop in New Zealand. All in all a great trip with a lot of sight seeing and pub crawls.

The only real incident I remember on this leg was in Melbourne. We were there for two shows, so on the morning of the second show Ralph, Pete from the band, and I all decided to go to Healesville Animal Sanctuary in the morning, as we weren't due at the gig until four in the afternoon. Healesville is about an hour outside the city, and one of the promoters' people with a van decided to take us. It was a great trip, but on the way back, on an infrequently used country road, we got a flat. No big deal, we have a spare, but it turned out, no tools. Here we were in the woods on a gig day with no tools to change our flat. This was also back when cell phones were not as common as they are now. One or two cars passed by, but no one stopped to help. After a while I tried getting the lug nuts off the tire with my Leatherman, which is a light duty multi tool I always carried. Ralph and I took turns working on the lug nuts and after about an hour, success. We were on our way to the gig, dirty, but not late.

Australia was great and New Zealand was beautiful. In Auckland we played a venue called The Supertop, which was an outdoor gig with a tent roof. And of course it rained. It rained hard with heavy winds. The tent started leaking; it was raining on us and coming in sideways. And as is always the case, the gig turned out to be a great one. This was our last show before heading back to the States. On the way home we would be stopping in Hawaii, for a week's vacation on Maui.

Shep, Alice's manager lived on Maui, so it was decided that anyone that wanted could stop there on the way home, and stay for a week. Condos were rented for us, and Shep had open house at his place every day. There was always food and drink, and his house was on the beach so the view was beautiful.

There was always something to do for those that wanted. One day Shep arranged for a sailboat for all of us. Another day was a luau at his place. It was just a great trip. Sitting on the beach in Maui I found myself again thinking back on the club days, and laughing to myself about where I was. It didn't seem real.

Time Off

After Australia and Hawaii we were going to have six or seven weeks off before heading to Europe. This was actually a good thing as I had been touring virtually non stop for about two and a half years. There was always a lot going on back home, and I was anxious to get back to the clubs.

One of the guys that kept me busy was Louie Appel, a drummer I had toured with a couple of years before. He was always playing with a lot of different people, and sometimes I would do gigs with him. These were nothing fancy gigs where we would throw his drums in my car and go do the gig. I never made more than a couple of bucks doing this, but I was doing it for fun and to keep busy more than anything else. I also met quite a few cool people with all the groups he played with. And it was with Louie that I did my one and only gig at the legendary CBGB's. That is one gig I will always be thankful for. It was just a hole in the wall, but it was a landmark.

Also at this time Al Pitrelli had a cover band that I would help out with once in a while, again more just for beer money than anything. He also had a couple of side projects that I would help out with. Another cool aspect of this time was that everyone in the local club scene knew each other. So when I went into a club I knew the bands that were playing and they knew me, and what tour I was on. The cool thing about this was that if a band didn't have a light guy or a sound guy, I could offer to jump in and help. And because they knew me they knew I could do it. I'd never ask for money when I did this, to me I was just paying back my good fortune. I started in these clubs.

Trash in Europe

Up until this point I had not yet been to Europe, so as always, I was looking forward to this trip. We would be going through Scandinavia as well.

The first show was in Denmark at the Midtfyns Festival. The show was going to have an estimated seventy thousand people in attendance. We went to the gig the day before to check it out, and it was big. There were kids in tents for miles around, waiting for the show. The next day our load in was six a.m., with a nine a.m. sound check. We had to do it that way because there were so many other bands setting up in front of us, and the show started in the early afternoon.

Sound check went fine and most of the band and crew went back to the hotel, as our show didn't start until eleven thirty that night. As usual, I stayed behind at the gig. I always loved festival shows and wanted to check out all the bands. That, and the fact that I didn't like to leave my gear unwatched. I was just more comfortable staying at the gig.

We did the gig that night and all went fine. The sun was just starting to go down, and the place was mayhem when Alice came out. By the time we got out of there it must have been three a.m., I felt like I was back in the clubs, just really big ones with catering and drivers. This was a great start to the European leg of the tour. Tomorrow we would be heading to Sweden. We would do festivals and our own shows in Sweden and Finland, and then we would be leaving Scandinavia and heading to Europe. First stop, Paris, France.

Europe Part Two

We flew into Paris and had that travel day and the next day off. We got into Paris late and just went out for drinks after checking into the hotel. I made sure not to overdo it, I wanted to get up and out early to go see the Louvre and a few other museums and historical sites. I wanted to head right out because whenever you try to coordinate a large group it just takes forever to get out the door. Whenever I went to a place I hadn't been to before, I always went with the assumption that I might never get back there, so I would always try to do all that I could.

I figured out the subway system that morning and was outside the Louvre by nine that morning. It really was amazing. Seeing the Mona Lisa in person was incredible. There were so many pieces of art that I had only seen in books, I couldn't believe that they were all here in one place. I did have one mishap though. I was walking around awestruck, just admiring all the artwork and wasn't paying attention to where I was walking. I felt a small raised surface in the floor that I took to be a loose brick or tile, and kept on walking. It was at this point that one of the museum guards started running toward me waving his arms and shouting in French. I had no idea what he was saying but I got the idea that I should look down.

I did look down and there it was, a two thousand year old Roman mosaic, and I was walking on it. Chalk up one more for the ugly American. I got off the mosaic and apologized as best I could. I didn't get tossed out, but I did get a lot of dirty looks the rest of my stay. I was to find out these would not be the only dirty looks I would get in France. In fact, I can't remember a trip to France that didn't include dirty looks from the locals.

I finished up my tour of the Louvre and headed back to the hotel. When I got to the lobby I ran into a few guys from the band and crew that were just heading out to sightsee. I hung with them the rest of the day; we went to the Eiffel Tower, Notre Dame and a few other places. These sites are truly amazing to see. It took forever to go all the way up to the top of Notre Dame, but it was worth it. We finished up our tour of Paris and headed back to the hotel.

After a shower and change of clothes everybody headed back to the lobby before we went out. The band had been invited out by the local record company people, and a few of the crew were heading over to a couple of local bars. While we were all hanging out waiting to leave, Ralph asked the band guys if he could go with them to the record label outing. The band told him that they were invited and couldn't bring anyone; it was a band only thing. Ralph didn't understand why he wasn't invited, so Derek the keyboard player explained it to Ralph as only he could. Let me explain first that by now, Derek knew how to push Ralphs buttons, and he enjoyed any chance he got.

To explain to Ralph why he couldn't go, Derek, with his most grandiose and pompous gesture, pointed to himself and said "Virtuoso" and then with a swirl and flash of his arm he pointed at Ralph and said "Virtually No So". As was usually the case Ralph got so mad he didn't know what to say. He just muttered a few things about kicking someone's ass. Not anything intelligible, it was just a few idle threats. We all laughed and the night was on.

The hotel we were staying at was on a five or six road intersection on a traffic circle. That meant in order to go to the bar just across the street; you had to navigate three of four busy street crossings. You might say no big deal, and you would be right. But after a long night of drinking you are taking your life in your hands. I will relate this next bit as it was told to me, as I have no recollection of these events myself.

Apparently, after leaving the bar after way too many drinks, I attempted to navigate the above mentioned course back to the hotel. I am told that there was not a streetlight or lamp post that I did not bounce off of. And furthermore there was not a local Frenchman that I also did not bump into. And I was also told that no matter which I bumped into, Frenchman or Lamp post, my response was the same. "F**k you Frenchie" was my battle cry that night. Personally, I find this hard to believe, but I can't argue with all the corroborating witnesses there were against me that night.

Getting to the hotel after navigating the obstacle course I realized that I left my jacket in the bar, so back I went, crashing through traffic and Frenchmen. I got to the bar, stole a beer from a friend, and crashed all the way back to the hotel. When I was told all this the next day, I asked my friends why they hadn't stopped me from stumbling through traffic a second time, nearly getting killed. Batty told me that a local bar patron said that I'd never make it back to the hotel without being run over, so bets were placed and they watched me from the windows of the bar like people at the horse track. I sure showed those locals. Batty made some money that night, and since he paid the bar tab I stumbled out on, we called it even.

The gig in Paris was a theater called Olympia. It was a long push down a cobble stone alleyway. Not a fun gig. The setup took a long time as there was not a lot of space to work. The load out took forever as well. A lot of these old theaters were built long before Rock and Roll, so they could be difficult.

Our next gig was going to be in Lyon, France. It was an old outdoor amphitheater amid ancient ruins. It was a much cooler and easier gig. After the shows in France it was off to Germany.

Guitar world at the Lyon gig

Pictures from the Lyon gig

103

The gig in Lyon, France

We traveled to Germany by tour bus, stopping first in Cologne and then Neunkirchen. Alice has always been big in Europe; the fans tend to be very loyal over there. The shows went over great; Alice and the band were in top form. After Germany it was a long bus ride to our next gig, Zagreb, Yugoslavia. It doesn't matter where you are, truck stops are all pretty much the same and on this run we saw a couple. We got into Zagreb late, and ended up grabbing a few drinks and something to eat near the hotel. There was not a whole lot around, times were tough in Yugoslavia. The gig went great as always and afterward we had another long bus ride to Greece for a show in Athens.

Load in for the Athens show was at three a.m. The idea was to get everything done early as it was going to get extremely hot later in the day. This really worked out well because we were set up so early most of us got to go to the old Greek ruins, which were not far away.

We were about fifteen minutes from the gig here

The gig in Athens was a big stadium; Alice was big in Greece also. After the crowd was let in Batty and I went out on stage with my camcorder to shoot the crowd and get them going. We really did get them going; they were pushing so hard they actually broke the barricade. Of course Batty and I took off, but we did let security know that their barricade was broken. With that info they realized that the barricade would not be sufficient for the show. There really wasn't much that could be done, but an escape route was established in case we lost the barricade and the stage got over run. Of course that didn't happen, the show was fine. It was a good load out and another long bus trip to Yugoslavia, Belgrade this time.

The Belgrade gig went well and it was time to head to the last show of this leg of the tour, Budapest, Hungary. This leg of the tour had been a lot of fun and I was sorry it was over. There were so many places I hadn't seen yet; I was hoping to come back soon. The day of the last gig I was determined to not get food poisoning. One thing I haven't touched on was that when I first started travelling a lot I got more than my share of food poisoning from local food and ice in my drinks. So on this last day I ate only dry bread and a banana, and guess what, by show time I needed a bucket to vomit in where I was working. On the road you don't get to call in when you are sick, there simply isn't anyone out there to do your job for you. We got through the show and I just got on the bus and crashed with no shower. We were driving straight through to Vienna to fly home to New York. By the time I got on the plane I felt a little better, but not completely. Not only was I still sick, I smelled from working in the heat with no shower. I'm sure I smelled bad because when Ralph sat next to me on the plane he told me I smelled and changed his seat. I can't say I blame him. After a while I started to feel better and managed to change clothes and get a sink shower in the bathroom. I just couldn't wait to get home. We would be home for a short time and then it was off to Japan.

One of the festivals we loaded into still trashed from the show the night before. You couldn't get away from the smell of urine and vomit if you tried. This picture was taken from stage and that tower is where the house sound board would go, with spotlights on the second level.

Trash in Japan

It was less than a year since I had been to Japan, so I felt like an old pro. We would have the same promoter, Mr. Udo, and I knew his people would be great. The gigs would all be fun and also, since the shows in Japan start by six or seven in the evening, we would be done by nine every night. This was perfect for going out and enjoying the Japanese nightlife.

I had told all the band guys to go see my friend George Silk while I was at the gig setting up the first show. They didn't have to be at the gig until late in the afternoon. They went to see George and told him that his adopted son Kenny Barr was in town and would be by to see him. On our way home from the gig we passed his shop and he had put my name on his welcome billboard, although he named me Kenny Barr Beer. I guess he was impressed with my beer drinking prowess when I had met him the year before. For the rest of my career with Alice, I have always been called Kenny Barr Beer.

George had insisted that we all come by for a barbeque. A lot of us went to his shop one day and ended up just hanging around drinking and talking. You just got drawn in by him. We did go back for a barbeque, which turned into an all day affair for some of us. I think George genuinely enjoyed hosting these events. We were eating and drinking on a little patch of grass next to a major roadway in the middle of Tokyo, and I felt completely at home. Later in the evening when we ran out of beer George handed me the keys to the shop and told me to get money out of the register and go buy more beer, which I did. By now it seemed normal to go get cash out of the register, there was no thought of theft on any of our minds. I guess there are some people you can become friends with right away.

One of the other high points of this leg of the tour had nothing to do with the shows, not really. By now the band and crew had been living and working together for a long time. One thing most of us had in common was a love of giving Ralph a hard time. This was nothing done with malice, just good natured fun. Ralph had given us so many catch phrases on this tour, he was in our minds all the time, and most of us would catch ourselves using these phrases without realizing it. It was nothing for someone to walk into a building and decree "This must be one of the Bigga Gigs", complete with hand gestures, and not realize it until they had done it.

The latest scheme to torment Ralph was when we instituted Ralph days. This was a well organized venture; notes would be put under the doors of people's hotel room doors letting them know that tomorrow was "Be nice to Ralph day". Ralph would get to the gig and everyone would go out of their way to greet him, get him something to drink, etc. Our Production Manager, Dan Stevenson, was a tough seasoned vet of the road, and he ran out to get Ralph his favorite fast food on Be Nice to Ralph Day. Of course Ralph was afraid to eat it, he didn't know what day it was and assumed that the food in the bag had been messed with. This went on all day and you could tell Ralph was getting annoyed, so we kept it up.

Next was Imitate Ralph Day, where we would all talk with the same heavy New York accent that Ralph had, and use his catch phrases a lot. "Bigga gigs" was thrown around so much that day I lost track. After that we had Be Mean to Ralph Day, where we would all talk to Ralph as though he had just insulted us. He came into the gig, and anyone he said good morning to would tell him to fuck off. And the insults got nastier as the day progressed. By now Ralph didn't know what to make of his situation.

After that was Ask Ralph Day. Everyone would go to Ralph and just ask him anything. The lighting guys would ask his advice on that days lighting focus. The sound guys asked his opinion on microphones and speaker placement. People would walk up to him and ask things like "What's the fastest land animal" or "Which ocean is the biggest". This wore on all day and you could see Ralph was getting frustrated, so of course we kept it up.

The final day was also the straw that broke the camels back. Our latest installment was Invisible Ralph Day, where we pretended we couldn't see him. When Batty, myself and Ralph got into the van to go to the gig, Batty and I started talking about Ralph as though he wasn't there, wondering where he was. Then we started talking bad about him, calling him lazy for missing the van to the gig, all the while with him sitting right there. I could tell he was starting to get mad, he had obviously had enough. When we got to the gig the rest of the crew all joined in. Invisible Ralph Day soon turned into Call Ralph a Lazy Piece of Crap While You're Standing Next to Him Pretending You Can't See Him Day. By lunch time Ralph had had enough, he came into catering and exploded. He called us all a lot of things I really don't want to print here.

Don't get me wrong, we deserved it. Ralph had put up with a lot of crap and we did get a little carried away. What we thought was good natured kidding had bothered him more than we thought it would. So we canceled the rest of the planned Ralph days and carried on with the tour. The rest of the shows went really well and we had a lot of fun. As on any tour sometimes bad things happen also. There were things that happened at the last show that I think we all could have done without. I don't think it merits details, just to let you know the road isn't all sunshine and roses. It's hard to live and work with people for any length of time. Anyway, time to head home, for a little while.

My tour laminate

Just outside my hotel in Japan

Beers were big in Japan

The End

The Trash tour was just about over. All we had left was a one off for Miller, a Halloween show. This tour had been a highpoint in my career and my life. I had been places I had never been, become part of the Alice Cooper family, and had helped to put on a show every night that I was proud of. By now I had no idea what my future with Alice Cooper would be. I had done a lot, worked in the studio on demos, helped with videos. I just hoped there would be another tour that involved this band and crew. And if you ever meet Ralph, ask him about when he stayed with me in L.A. while I was working in the studio with Alice and the band. He does a great impression of my drunken antics, and I'm sure he would welcome the chance to get back at me after telling stories about him.

The Miller Halloween Show

Rules of the Road:

When making new friends always ask for two forms of picture identification to make sure they are of legal age.

Failing to do this can result in prison time, lawsuits, gunplay, and the loss of all your civil liberties.

Always insist on two forms of picture I.D.!!

Joe Lynn Turner

One of the local side projects I got involved with was Joe Lynn Turner. He had been the singer in Rainbow, and he was playing east coast shows on his own. Al Pitrelli was his guitar player and that's how I ended up doing shows with him. Joe was a total rock star and not in a bad way. He was easily one of the best singers I have ever seen and he just had a star quality about him.

We mostly played clubs around New York, New Jersey and Connecticut, all driving distance from home. The gigs were all one offs where we would all just drive in and do the show. The band were mostly comprised of guys I knew, John O'Reilly on drums, Greg Smith on bass, Gary Corbett on keyboards, and Al. When Al stopped doing shows I stayed on and the new guitar player was Karl Cochran. Everyone in the band was a great player, and between the classic rock songs and the newer JLT material, it was an amazing show. This was a total back to my roots experience for me. And since I could tech for any of these guys, a lot of the time I was the only crew.

Joe has done a lot of gigs and records in the past few years. If you have the opportunity to go see him or pick up a cd, do it. You won't be disappointed. If I was still able I would love to do those shows with him again.

Anything is Possible

As had become my norm, as soon as I got home from the Alice tour I was to start rehearsals for the next Debbie Gibson tour, although by now she was called Deborah. Her new record was called "Anything is Possible" and it was definitely going to broaden her audience. The songs were geared to a more adult market than her previous records. She had brought in big name production people and made a record she could be proud of.

Rehearsals were at a studio in Brooklyn, and except for one player the band was all new. The new band were all seasoned professionals and were very low maintenance. Rehearsals were just a matter of babysitting and prepping gear for the tour. We would be in Brooklyn for a while and then go to L.A. for production rehearsals with the full stage, lights and sound. Rehearsals were easy, nearly boring at this point.

We ran through our time in Brooklyn and before I knew it we were in Los Angeles working. Which was great for me, I got to introduce my backline partner John to Barnies Beanery. I was becoming quite the regular there. Production rehearsals also went really well. There was one incident I recall that took place at a bar not far from the hotel. A few of us were drinking and by now John and I were like brothers, and had started to get on each others nerves. In our drunken stupor we decided to settle things outside. Don't ask me why, it seemed like a good idea at the time. As we squared off I never thought it was going to actually come to punches, and the next thing I knew, Wham! Johnny was in good shape and had punched me in the jaw so hard I saw stars. Even drunk I didn't want this to escalate, so I called John and idiot and tried to walk back in the bar, but by now he felt bad and insisted I hit him back. So I did. We both went back in the bar with bloody faces and kept on drinking. The rest of the crew were a little taken aback by this, but we weren't fazed. We had worked it out and it was over.

I thought I was done with this section, but I just got an e mail from John Karlquist and he reminded me of another story from this time period. We were rooming together and he had mentioned to me an actress he had met the last time he was in L.A. He had played a small part in one of Deborah's videos and he met the actress on the set. They must have hit it off because she gave John her number and asked him to call her when he got back to L.A. When John told me this I was stunned that he hadn't made the call. I even insisted he do so, I did a lot of insisting back then. I don't know why but he didn't want to, so I kept at him. After days of giving him verbal grief I decided on another course of action.

This particular day I was wearing grey sweat socks, one with a blue stripe, and I told John that I was going to wear those socks until he called the actress. This became known as the blue and grey event. I stuck to my guns; I would work, sleep and go out in those socks. The only time they came off my feet was when I showered. It did get bad, after a few days the socks started to feel like they were made of raw liver. And the smell was ungodly, I couldn't stand it myself. There was a time we were with some other crew riding in a car and someone said"Ughh, there must be a garbage dump nearby", but I knew it was me. I have to admit that after five or six days I was getting ready to cave, I thought I was getting a fungus and the smell was more than I could handle. Thankfully, John caved before I did and he made the call. It felt so good to get those socks off. I don't remember if we threw them out the window or burned them. I don't know what happened with John and the actress, I was just glad that the blue and grey incident was behind me.

Another night we were all at the hotel and the party in my room ran out of beer. We knew some of the other crew had a stash, so we had to get into their rooms. Now as all the rooms had balconies; all you had to do to get to the next room was climb over your balcony railing, jump to the next balcony and climb over their railing. It sure seemed simple enough. John and I went out on a mission, we made it to the next room over and it was locked. We had to keep going and hope that if we found an open room, that it was someone we knew. We didn't seem to notice that our rooms were on the second floor of the hotel, we were really high up jumping around like Spiderman.

This went on for a little while before my luck finally ran out. I grabbed for a railing and it was loose. I lost my grip and down I went, but not to the ground, I landed on an aluminum storage shed. Where I made impact with the roof it had caved in quite a bit, and as I tried to stand and climb down it continued to collapse around me. I couldn't get good footing, the roof just kept buckling until it finally gave way and I went through the roof and landed on the hotels lawn maintenance equipment. Yeah, that one hurt. I stumbled around and finally got out and made my way back to the hotels front door.

I looked pretty much like I just done all the things I had just done. My clothes were torn; I was bleeding, dirty and half drunk. I tried to look as innocent as possible as I asked the front desk clerk for another key to my room. I can't imagine what she was thinking, but she gave me another key. By the time I got back upstairs John had scored more beer, so we were back in business. I'm pretty sure I stayed off the balcony for the remainder of my stay, but I won't swear to it. Oh, and the garden shed was totaled, it looked like the Hulk had thrown a super villain through it. In case you're wondering, aluminum sheds went for four hundred dollars back then. I bought one, I know.

Next was off to Rio de Janeiro, to play the Rock in Rio festival. This was a huge event with a lot of bands. Our hotel was right on the beach and Rio was beautiful. A lot of bands and crews were staying at the same hotel, so I ran into a lot of people I knew. This was going to be a paid vacation. The festival was already going on when we got there. All we had to do was show up with our band gear and put it on rolling risers. This was one of those gigs where you only had a few minutes to get set up, so you would pre-set on risers off stage.

The crowd was enormous and Deborah and the band played really well. This was to be the first stop on a full world wide tour, and it could not have gone better. We finished the show and packed up, back to the hotel for a night out. Rio was really a great place to go out and tear it up. Everyone was in a good party mood, the first show had gone well and we were looking at a long tour with more of the same. Or so we thought.

I'm not sure if it was before or after we left Rio, but we were all told that the tour was off, indefinitely. I guess there were things going on behind the scenes that we didn't know about. Most road crews are never involved with record label type of business, so if the label isn't supporting a record, or if anything else comes up that could derail a tour, we're the last to know. So it was back home with no job. There was talk that the tour would be worked out eventually, but there was no way to tell when.

I started to make some phone calls to round up work and found out that it wouldn't be long before Alice Cooper was starting up again. There would be new band guys, so there was no way to know if I had a job or not. There was always the chance that the new band guys would already have their own techs. So I had two maybes, the Gibson tour and The Coop. I kept making calls hoping something would turn up, and like always, it did.

Deborah had scheduled a tour of the Pacific Rim, which worked out perfect. I had been confirmed for the next Alice tour which would start up right after I got home. We started rehearsals with Deborah and everything was on track, until there was the possibility of extending her short tour. There was talk of doing a benefit that I wouldn't be able to do, it conflicted with some of the tour dates on the Alice Cooper tour I had already confirmed. There was no way to know if this benefit would happen, so I had to bow out of the tour as I couldn't finish it. It worked out well though, my friend Nick Morley was brought in to replace me, and the Alice Cooper people brought me out to L.A. six weeks early to do the rehearsals. Sometimes things do come together.

One of my first tour laminates

Back with the Coop

Alice's new record was called "Hey Stoopid", and it was getting serious support from the record label. There were a lot of guest stars that played on it, Slash, Joe Satriani, Steve Vai, Ozzy did back up vocals. There was a big buzz going on around this record.

Rehearsals would be in L.A. for a few weeks, just me and the band. I would baby-sit them while they played, making sure they had whatever they needed. When they weren't playing I would help with their gear, helping them get whatever they needed to do the tour. There were some changes in the band, only Eric Singer and Derek Sherinian were back. On guitar there was Stef Burns and Vinnie Moore. On bass we had Greg Smith, a fellow Long Islander. Greg had played the same bar circuit that I had worked for years, and as a result we knew a lot of the same people.

The work schedule was pretty routine; we were set up in the same studio the whole time. The guys had a schedule that they kept for playing, and I did any other prep work around that. Those of us from out of town all stayed in the same place, although I don't remember hanging out with the guys when we were home. I remember Vinnie liked to practice a lot. I think that any time we were at the apartments he was playing. He was one of those incredibly fast shredder type players. He could play things you just couldn't believe. The rehearsals went along pretty quietly; the band just got the work done.

The tour would be starting out in the States. Alice had been booked on the "Operation Rock & Roll" tour.

Also on the bill were Judas Priest, Motorhead, Dangerous Toys and Metal Church. This tour would be a real head bangers dream. Priest and Alice both had considerable stages, so coordinating them was important. After rehearsals with the band we moved to a soundstage and rehearsed the show on the tour stage set. This stage was utilizing both drum and keyboard risers that had to be moved on and off stage quickly. To facilitate this, I made sure that all the keyboard gear was bolted down, and the drum tech would do the same. I was able to setup the keyboards out of the way, and when the riser was ready to go on or off stage I would just ride with it while it was being fork lifted into place. The first time Derek saw this process I did hear him groan, there was always the ever present fear of the equipment falling and him losing everything. That never happened, but there were a few close calls.

After all the kinks were worked out it was time to head out and meet up with the rest of the tour. We would be working with the Priest crew to figure out the choreography of getting each others gear on and off stage, which took a lot of doing. We made it happen although space and time would both get very tight.

The show would start in the early afternoon; it had to with all the bands that were playing. Metal Church was up first, followed by Dangerous Toys. Both these bands were good, I would check out their show whenever I could. Next up was Motorhead, and I always tried to watch them. I would usually be working on guitars when they were waiting to go on, and Lemmy would usually stop by and shoot the breeze. He's a true Metal die hard and he's got a lot of cool stories going all the way back to his days with Jimi Hendrix.

Most days Alice went on after Motorhead, but there were exceptions. After our show Priest was up. Those guys rocked hard every night. They had been touring on their latest record "Painkiller" for over a year and they were at the top of their game. They had the drum riser that opened up in front and their singer Rob Halford would ride out on his motorcycle. The crowd went wild every night. Rob always had the audience in the palm of his hand. He and Alice are two of the best front men I have ever seen. And Judas Priest as a band was just perfect every night. All the guys played really well, and I never saw them have a bad gig. Even at the last show when Rob got injured, the band played on. And after a song or two, Rob was back on stage injury and all, and delivered as good a show that night as any other.

Once the tour got up and running things smoothed out pretty well. There were a few incidents here and there, but nothing tragic or too embarrassing.

Post Op

After the tour with Priest we headed home. We would have a little time off before heading to Europe. It was at this time that Alice and the band made their appearance in the movie "Wayne's World", which turned out to be a big hit.

Before heading overseas we would also be doing a short promo tour. These would be shows with Alice and the band. The shows were in parking lots, record stores, in the street. Every gig was different. The crew consisted of me and Eric's drum tech Chris. We would go to these different gigs and do the best we could. We showed up at a record store where we were supposed to play on the roof, overlooking the crowd. When we got to load in I checked it out and just didn't think the roof was safe. The initial thought was to just do a meet and greet, but when Toby, a member of management got there, we saw a place at the back of the store that would work. So we went for it. The band and Alice rocked the place. There were kids sitting on CD displays, hanging from the rafters, trashing the place. And everyone loved it, including the record store owner. This was good press for everyone. After the show the guys signed autographs before they took off, everyone left happy. The streets were so crowded with fans that the bus had to keep circling the block, and as we made it out of the store you would hop on the bus as it went by. The whole promo tour was like this. Alice played right on the street in Times Square in New York and stopped traffic. This was a great sendoff before heading over to Europe.

Stoopid in Europe

For this leg of the tour a few significant changes had been made. First, Vinnie Moore had decided to leave and we were lucky enough to get a guitar player from the previous tour, Pete Freezin'. The second change was that Eric's drum tech had also left the tour. And because he left on short notice there was no time to hire a replacement and get the necessary work visas. At the time I didn't realize the impact this would have on my career, but it had a big one. There will be more on that later. We ended up getting a friend of Battys' to drum tech, a guy named Pedro. He was a good guy, just more of a colorful character than a tech. On one long ferry ride he got drunk and decided that no one could use the stairs without a backstage pass. This applied to all the passengers on board. He had decreed the back stage line and wouldn't listen to anyone. When the tour manager tried to talk to him, Pedro threatened him with knuckle sandwiches. We ended up just leaving him alone until he passed out.

Anyway, back to the tour. We were in Europe rehearsing at Wembley Arena. Our support band on this leg was a band out of the U.K. called "The Almighty". They were a good hard rock band and a bunch of fun guys to hang out with. I think they are responsible for at least one of my cases of alcohol poisoning.

The tour started out in the U.K., which was great, I love it there. Alice was still really popular and The Almighty was a hot up and coming band. This was a great bill for the tour.

Before I go any further let me tell you a little about the actual show. As always the guys in the band were good players and they hit it hard every night. Alice was Alice, singer and theatrical front man who also hit it hard. I have seen the Coop playing outdoors in the driving cold rain, and he never missed a beat. There was never any talk of cutting songs or shortening the show. It was as if we were working in perfect conditions.

On this tour we also used the living screen, which was a movie screen that Alice could walk into, and when he did he was in the movie on screen. This was a great effect and I'm surprised the entertainment industry hasn't utilized it more. There were parts of this segment where demons or monsters would break out and run from the movie, onto the stage. The crowd went wild for this every night.

We also had a piece of equipment that we called the Frankenstein table. There was a segment where a photographer would take pictures of Alice, annoying him. The photographer was always played by our wardrobe girl Kelli. Did I forget to mention that when you work for Alice anyone on the crew is subject to being part of the show? Over the years I was part of the street gang during "Gutter Cats", a segment where a street gang came onstage and rumbled with Alice and the band. Anyway Alice would send the boys over to grab Kelli and she would be strapped down and covered, the table would fly out into the lighting rig. When it came back down there was a disfigured dummy where Kelli had been. It was another crowd pleaser. The show really did have a lot of unique theatrical moments.

CALLING: FROM → / TO ↑

FROM \ TO	Austria	Belgium	Denmark	France	Ireland	Israel	Italy	Netherlands	Norway	Spain	Sweden	Switzerland	United Kingdom	United States	W. Germany	Finland
Austria	00	0032	0045	0033	00353	00972	0039	0031	0047	0034	0046	0041	0044	001	0049	00358
Belgium	0043		0045	0033	00353	00972	0039	0031	0047	0034	0046	0041	0044	001	0049	00358
Denmark	00943	00932		00933	009353	009972	00939	00931	00947	00934	00945	00941	00944	0091	00949	009358
France	1943	1932	1945		19353	19972	1939	1931	1947	1934	1946	1941	1944	191	1949	19358
Ireland	1643	1632	1645	633		16972	1639	1631	1647	1634	1646	1641	1644	161	1649	16358
Isreal	0043	0032	0045	0033	00353		0039	0031	0047	0034	0046	0041	0044	001	0049	00358
Italy	0043	0032	0045	0033	00353	00972		0031	0047	0034	0046	0041	0044	001	0049	00358
Netherlands	09-43	09-32	09-45	09-33	09-353	09-972	09-39		09-47	09-34	09-46	09-41	09-44	09-1	09-49	09-358
Norway	09543	09532	09545	09533	095353	095972	09539	09531		09534	09546	09541	09544	0951	09549	095358
Spain	0743	0732	0745	0733	07353	07972	0739	0731	0747		0746	0741	0744	071	0749	07358
Sweden	00943	00932	00945	00933	009353	009972	00939	00931	00947	00934		00941	00944	001	00949	009358
Switzerland	0043	0032	0045	0033	00353	00972	0039	0031	0047	0034	0046		0044	001	0049	00358
United Kingdom	01043	01032	01045	01033	010353	010972	01039	01031	01047	01034	01046	01041		0101	01049	010358
United States	01143	01132	01145	01133	011353	011972	01139	01131	01147	01134	01146	01141	01144		01149	011358
West Germany	0043	0032	0045	0033	00353	00972	0039	0031	0047	0034	0046	0041	0044	001		00358
Finland	99043	99032	99045	99033	990353	990972	99039	99031	99047	99034	99046	99041	99044	9901	99049	

Before everyone carried a cell phone, itineraries included country code info for phone calls

The Joe Elliott Story

This is a story I have told many times over the years, and it usually gets a laugh, so I decided to include it. It's a good example of how cocky and oblivious people can be. And when I say people, of course I am talking about myself.

There were a bunch of us, band and crew hanging out. I'm not sure if it was a hotel lobby or somewhere else, but wherever it was there were long benches on three sides that we were all sitting on. I guess sort of like a glass enclosed patio with seating all around. Anyway, as I said we were hanging out and there were a lot of people coming and going, a constant influx to talk to. Suddenly, the most beautiful girl I had ever seen sat next to me and she had the most amazing mini skirt on that I had ever seen. Since she had chosen to sit with me, my mid twenties brain deduced that she must want to hook up with me. Why else would she sit there?

Armed with this information I proceeded to introduce myself and offer her a drink. I spent the better part of a half hour putting on all my best moves, trying to be charming. Not only was she beautiful, she had a great personality and I was having a good time just talking. After a while she said she had to go. She very politely shook my hand and said it was a pleasure meeting me, and off she went. This threw my mid twenties brain for a loop. I thought all this was a done deal, and she was gone. This made no sense.

We continued to hang out for a bit and then headed out to go to a pub. As we were leaving one of the band guys made a comment on what a nice guy Joe

Elliott was. I asked where they had seen him; I had always been a fan of his band, Def Leppard. That's when they dropped the bomb on me. I think it was Pete that told me. He said "He was sitting on the other side of that hot girl you were trying to pick up. Oh, by the way, that was his wife." I really didn't have much to say after that. Sorry Joe.

There was another night about this time on the tour where I went out to dinner with Eric Singer, just to hang out. He had played on the KISS record "Revenge" and was originally going to be uncredited. But when Eric Carr got sick again and eventually passed away, there was a feeling that Eric Singer might be in the band.

We talked about a lot of things that night and I got the feeling there was something important on Eric's mind. He asked me what I was doing after the Alice tour and I told him what I had lined up. I asked him what he was doing, and eventually he told me that he might be the next drummer in KISS, although nothing was definite. Later he asked me if I would be interested in being his drum tech if he got the gig, and of course I told him yes. I had known Eric a long time and I respected him as a person and a player. I also considered him a good friend. I think Eric wanted to have a tech locked in before he got the gig, so he could bring in who he wanted, not end up with someone the band knew. On tour I started taking a lot of pictures of Eric's drums so I would be familiar when the time came.

Some of the pictures I took of Eric's drums

Shoe Beers

I think this next story takes place in Belgium. It was a night out in a place I won't forget. There were a few of us that went out for dinner and then, what a surprise, went looking for a pub. As we were walking we found a cool looking place that served the big yard ale glasses of beer. This looked like the right place for us. We went in and sat at a table, when the barman came by and took our order, he put his hand out like he was expecting something. I took out money, thinking he wanted to get paid upfront, but he shook his head no. He pointed to a sign on the wall and a basket hanging from the ceiling. He wanted a shoe from each of us as collateral, so that we wouldn't steal the big yard ale glasses.

We all thought this was hilarious and each gave him a shoe. He took them, put them in the basket, and hoisted them up to the ceiling. He then went and got our beer. There we were at the table, drinking large beers with one shoe on each. That was fine until you needed to use the bathroom. We inquired about borrowing a shoe back to walk to the toilet, but he wasn't having it. It was beer or shoe, but not both. Of course we chose beer, and just walked through the dirty wet bar into the even dirtier and wetter bathroom. What can you do? When we wanted another beer we would ask him for another "Shoe Beer". That's what we named them, and the place became the "Shoe Beer Bar". This went on until we hit the limit of what he would sell us. He gave us the check, and it wasn't until the check was paid that the basket was lowered and we got our shoes back.

The sign at the "Shoe Beer Bar"

Our shoes as collateral

Still Stoopid

The tour was rolling along pretty well. By now we had been through England, Ireland, Scotland, Belgium, Holland, Switzerland, Germany, France and we still had Norway, Denmark, Sweden and Finland to go. We were doing good shows with a great support act. The crew had gelled really well and both gig days and days off were always fun. We were rolling into Norway with a couple of days off before our show. We usually stayed in good hotels near a lot of stuff to do, and this was no exception. There were a lot of good clubs and bars nearby which we made full use of. A lot of the locals knew who we were, so there were usually a lot of drinks being bought. There was one rock club, Elm Street, where most of us hung out a lot.

The Almighty were also staying nearby and I saw them at Elm Street all the time. As things in Oslo could be expensive they had struck a deal with the club. If the club would cover their drinks for the days off, the band would come over to Elm Street after opening for Alice in the arena and play for free, which they did. I did mooch a lot of drinks from their tab. As soon as we were done loading out after our show, I went over with my girlfriend Nina, who lived in Norway, and watched The Almighty. It was a fun club show where they screwed around with cover songs and anything else they felt like playing.

These last few gigs in Scandinavia were a really good time. Late nights on the bus, I ended up on The Almighty's bus more than a few times. We had all become good friends and this was another tour I was sorry to see end.

Rules of the Road:

A strippers job is to separate you from your money.

Never buy a stripper a drink; you'll be paying $25 for ginger ale.

Most strippers are crazy.

Most strippers are not working their way through college, law school, med school, etc.

If you leave the club with a stripper, insist on going to your hotel*. If you go to her place there will always be a pissed off room mate, a kid with a cold, or a broken appliance they'll be trying to get you to look at.

If you're in town for a couple of days, never go back to the club where you hooked up with a stripper the night before and go home with a different one. Stripper #1 will show up at your hotel pissed at stripper #2 and you. This will be the one instance where two strippers in your hotel room will be a bad thing.

*Provided you have secured your possessions as previously described.

NAMM

After we got home from the tour with the Coop, Eric was offered the gig with KISS, and plans were being made. I was confirmed as his new drum tech and the two of us started talking a lot about what we needed to do to be ready. This was an important gig for both of us, and we wanted to make sure everything went well. As part of that, we decided that I would fly out to California for the NAMM show.

The NAMM show is the National Association of Music Merchants, a big trade show for anyone in the music industry. Eric wanted me to meet all his endorsers, as I would be dealing with them while I was his tech. The plan was that I would fly out to L.A., he would pick me up and I would just stay at his place. As I said earlier, we were friends first, and co-workers second.

All went as planned; I met the reps from Eric's drum and cymbal companies, and saw a lot of old faces as well. The trip had been worth all the effort, I felt a little more prepared for my new job. And as with most things in my life there was a little side adventure while I was out there. After my first day at Eric's house he casually mentioned that one of the original cast members from Star Trek lived across the street. He thought I already knew, he did know what a fan I was. From then on whenever we were home I was usually looking out the window waiting for his neighbor to come out. It was a little "Fatal Attraction" "Star Trek" style. And with all that, I never saw him.

Revenge

The new KISS record, the one Eric had played on was called "Revenge". Rehearsals were starting a couple of months after I had gone out for the NAMM show. As a kid I had been a big fan of the band, so I was really familiar with their music. This came in handy because on this tour Eric would also be singing back up. But his style of drumming didn't really make it possible to have a stationary vocal microphone stand, and he was never comfortable with a headset microphone either. The solution was for me to swing the microphone over to him when he needed it, and quickly swing it out when he was done. If you see any close up footage from the tour, you'll see me up there with him.

The first day of rehearsals I was the new guy, the rest of the crew were veterans and they and the band all had a history. When I first walked into the rehearsal room, Paul came right over and introduced himself. When I walked over to say hello to Gene, Eric told him that I was his drum tech, and his response was to look me dead in the eye and ask "Why"? I had nothing, I wasn't sure what to say, I think I just shrugged my shoulders and headed over to the drum kit. The rest of the crew were all cool, Romeo, Spike and T-Byrd had already been there at rehearsals.

I got through the first day OK, which is always the hardest. When you start a new job with a group you've never worked with before, you never really know what to expect. So I was glad the first day was over and I could start getting into a normal routine.

Club Tour

The first leg of the KISS "Revenge" tour was going to be a club tour in the States, followed by a couple of arenas in the U.K. I think that the general idea was to break in the new member and also create a buzz. KISS playing clubs made the news wherever we went, and created a lot of mayhem at each gig. The shows were fun and there was a little less stress than if we played arenas. I don't know how Eric felt, but I was glad that my first KISS shows were done this way.

There were gigs that were difficult, some of the road cases we had didn't physically fit through the doors of some clubs. You had to unload them outside and hand carry your gear in. This was especially true for me; Eric's road cases were enormous. I would try to get the stagehands to all make one trip together, the big fear was having something get stolen. It was also tight quarters doing shows this way.

During the gig I was always on the drum riser with Eric, taking care of the microphone and fixing anything that might break during the show. At a few of these gigs our eight foot by eight foot riser had to be set up against the back wall on stage to save room. This meant that I was just to Eric's left, close enough to have a conversation during the whole show. I would crouch and stay low profile, but there were a few gigs where I got hit by a drumstick, there just wasn't enough room. We got through it though; we have always worked well together.

We started the tour in California, with a show in San Francisco before heading back to L.A. to do two nights at The Troubadour. These shows were already getting all the attention that they could. People came out in droves to see KISS in a club. Here we were playing clubs with basically an arena crew. Most club tours are lucky to have a couple of guys, but we had a full backline crew, monitor and front of house engineers, sound and light crew, buses, semi trucks. KISS doesn't do anything small, even in clubs.

We also had a production manager, Charlie Hernandez, who is one of the top guys in the field. I don't think that there's a major tour out there that he's not working with. I was glad for the chance to work with him because once you prove yourself; he can help keep you busy for the rest of your career.

After California we worked our way east, first through Texas and then Georgia. The shows were going well and I was starting to fit in with the other crew guys. I had actually known Paul's tech T-Byrd from the clubs in New York. He was a sound guy back then and we had done gigs together here and there. From Georgia we headed north, first to Baltimore and Philadelphia and on to Canada. By now the whole tour was in a groove and the ship was sailing smoothly along. After Canada it was down to Boston and finally to New York for two shows. There is nothing like a New York audience at a KISS show. We would be doing one show in Manhattan at The Ritz and a show in Brooklyn, at L'Amour. The shows went well, and after New York it was off to the U.K. for some arena shows.

Revenge in the U.K.

When we went out to the U.K. to do bigger venues (Bigga Gigs), the band hadn't finalized the look of the new stage show. They wanted to get out and play, so it was decided that these first arena gigs would be done on the set from their previous tour "Hot in the Shade", which was the sphinx design. So there would be some set up and rehearsal time when we got to the first arena in Scotland.

Setting up at Wembley Arena, England

On the arena stage there was finally enough room for Eric to play without worrying about me being in his way. The bigger stage worked out well right from the start, and after putting all our gear into clubs, being back in an arena was like going home. I guess things had changed. And these gigs were fun also, because some of the old Long Island Mafia was with the support act. It was good to have done arena shows with KISS, now I was really looking forward to the tour on the new stage.

140

Revenge Tour

The Revenge tour was going to start in Pennsylvania, with rehearsals at the arena we would be playing first. This was a typical arrangement, setting up and working out the kinks in the arena where you would start the tour. Since I lived in New York, only about two hours from the arena, I had made arrangements for my friend John Karlquist to drive me and my road cases to the gig. It was easier for me to do it that way, and John got to check out the new stage set and also make a couple of dollars. As he didn't have a vehicle big enough, we used my big old pick up truck, which was a local legend itself from all our adventures. If I ever do a book giving more detail to the club days, the old truck will be all over it.

The Legendary Truck

Anyway, my tools and I had been dropped off and it was on with another tour. I think there was more to this production than I had worked with before. This tour had the Statue of Liberty, which blew up and became a Terminator. There was a ton of pyro and lights, a cool stage with cabinets all over. As KISS had always tried to stay out on the road, I had figured this would be my gig for quite a while.

As I said earlier the stage had speaker cabinets all over it, like there had been an earthquake or some disaster. We had the Statue of Liberty, which was right behind the drum riser where I worked. Between the drum riser and old lady liberty was a large laser unit. Back then the laser generators were enormous and required very high voltage to power them, and a constant flow of water to cool them. It was definitely a potentially dangerous combination. These lasers were not only powerful enough to shoot to the back of the arena, they could sear flesh also. During one set up I was working on the drums, and the laser tech was behind me focusing lasers. Time constraints were such that we had to work at the same time, safe or not. While I was working our monitor engineer looked over at me and said "hey dude, your head is smoking". I reached behind my head and felt that my hair had been burned; I guess the laser had just gotten to my scalp. I have a tiny cauterized spot on the back of my head as a souvenir. It was just another typical work day.

One of the other features of the tour included strippers that would come out and strip tease during one of Paul's songs. The song was about taking it off, so this seemed like a natural choice to accompany the band. Initially this was put into the bands tour rider, the document that goes to each local promoter specifying what the band needs for the gig. At first things went OK. The girls would show up and be instructed by our production manager on what they were supposed to do, and how far they could go. Sometimes the girls were hot; sometimes they were not so hot. I can remember being on the drum riser with Eric craning my neck to see the nightly strippers. And then there were the girls in those little nowhere towns that really shouldn't have been stripping. They should have been at a weight watchers meeting or a cosmetic surgeon. Some were so bad you couldn't wait for the song to be over, and this was supposed to be a high point of the show. It didn't take too many of these farm animal events before the band decided they needed to get three hot strippers and have them travel with us. This didn't go over too well with anyone's wife or girlfriend. None of them thought too much of the idea of their partner on a tour bus with three strippers. Fortunately for me, they rode a different bus. They seemed OK, but I don't think I ever spoke to any of them even once; there was no time for interaction. At least there was consistency for the audience although most of the crew lost interest in this segment of the show.

Another part of the tour that worked out well was the opening acts. One was Great White, who I had worked with before. Also for one run we had Faster Pussycat. I heard Trixter was going to be on the tour and that was good, two of the Long Island Mafia, Howie and Todd, were on their crew. They introduced me to the band and they all seemed pretty cool, although they were really young. There was always a lot of hanging out together and on more than one night I ended up crashing on their bus for the ride.

One of the other tour effects that didn't always cooperate was old Lady Liberty herself. During one song the outer layer was supposed to blow off and reveal a terminator underneath. This was a cool effect, when it worked. There were a lot of nights when the outer pieces would get hung up and one of the set carpenters would have to climb up there and start kicking them off one by one. I don't suppose that was the look the designers were going for.

There was another gig on the tour where the ceiling height didn't allow for one of the bottom sections to be used. Now the Statue of Liberty was constructed a certain way, with stability in mind. It was only meant to be put together with all its sections. But on the road you sometimes have to adapt and make things happen, the statue was a centerpiece of the show, we had to have it. Lady Liberty was put up, minus the bottom section and secured as well as possible, she appeared safe. The show started as usual and all appeared fine, as least where I was on stage.

What I didn't know until later was that when the show started kicking into high gear, concussion mortars and high volume rattling the building, Lady Liberty started to lean forward, toward the stage. Namely, she was leaning in the direction of the drum riser with Eric and me on it. Earlier I mentioned that the laser unit was between us, so if she had toppled we would have had the crushing impact, and also high voltage flowing through a running water supply.

When the problem was first spotted our stage manager scrambled to do what he could. He saw a forklift and had it brought over to the base of the statue. The force and weight of the lift was enough to keep the base of the statue from kicking back any more, she was secure. When I found all this out after the show I asked the stage manager why they didn't tell me that this was going on, so we could have been ready to vacate the drum riser. He said "I didn't want to worry you". I couldn't argue with that.

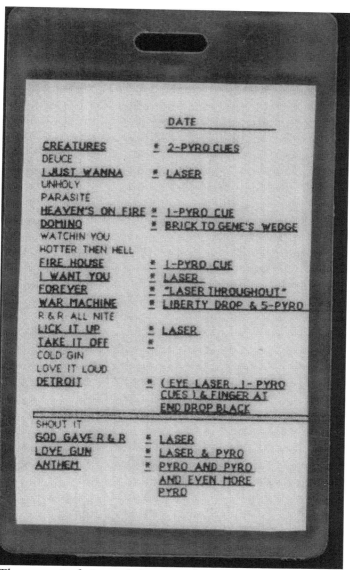

DATE _____

CREATURES   * 2-PYRO CUES
DEUCE
I JUST WANNA   * LASER
UNHOLY
PARASITE
HEAVEN'S ON FIRE * 1-PYRO CUE
DOMINO   * BRICK TO GENE'S WEDGE
WATCHIN YOU
HOTTER THEN HELL
FIRE HOUSE   * 1-PYRO CUE
I WANT YOU   * LASER
FOREVER   * "LASER THROUGHOUT"
WAR MACHINE   * LIBERTY DROP & 5-PYRO
R & R ALL NITE
LICK IT UP   * LASER
TAKE IT OFF   *
COLD GIN
LOVE IT LOUD
DETROIT   * (EYE LASER , 1- PYRO
                       CUES) & FINGER AT
                       END DROP BLACK
SHOUT IT
GOD GAVE R & R   * LASER
LOVE GUN   * LASER & PYRO
ANTHEM   * PYRO AND PYRO
                       AND EVEN MORE
                       PYRO

*The pyro tech issued the crew laminates with pyro
and laser cues on them for our own safety*

145

Bigga Gigs Be Gone

I just went into the other room to do something, trying to figure out my next pages here. Suddenly it hit me, there was a funny Ralph story on this tour, and he wasn't even on it. It has been a while since I told one of his stories, so here goes.

At one of the arenas either Howie or Todd from the Trixter crew made up a wanted poster of Ralph, just to be funny. By now his expression "Bigga Gigs" was used by everyone on the tour. They put things on the poster to be funny, things like "Answers to Hey You", it was nothing mean, just making fun. They made copies of these and put them all over the stage area, even up by Eric's drum monitor. We all laughed about it and proceeded to start the show.

Trixter was up first and they started their set as usual. About half way into their first song the bass player, P.J., broke a string. Breaking a bass string is very unusual as they are very heavy and thick. This on its own was no big deal, but the band continued to have technical difficulties throughout their set. We all noticed and thought it odd, but sometimes that's just how the night goes. They had issues with their wireless systems; I think one of their amps failed. This was one of the all time record breaking gear breaking nights I had ever seen.

When KISS hit the stage it didn't take long for the night's bad mojo to hit us. There were some microphone issues and monitor issues, which can happen. But then Eric broke a cymbal during the first song, and it was less than one song later that his bottom snare head blew out. A bottom snare head breaking, especially one on a well maintained drum is even rarer than a bass string breaking. After we changed out the snare drum Eric pointed at the poster of Ralph and said "Get that f***in' thing out of here", which I did. We all gathered the posters up and got them off stage, making sure the entire area was clear. It sounds stupid now, but we were all convinced that it would be a hell night if even one poster was nearby.

And as if by some miracle, the rest of the night went fine. Once the posters were removed the rest of the show went smoothly. Here and there I could see other guys on the crew shaking their heads and laughing. There was a big sense of relief among us.

After the gig a few of us went to the production office and called Ralph to yell at him for ruining our gig. He didn't know what we were talking about; he was home and I think we woke him up. Obviously it wasn't his fault, we just wanted to vent and he was our unwilling target.

In order to break the bad mojo, our production manager Tim gathered up the posters, put them in a pile, and burned them. A few of us danced around them, like American Indians, chanting "Bigga Gigs Be Gone, Bigga Gigs Be Gone". Our dance included the official Bigga Gigs hand gestures that I described earlier. It seems to have worked; I still haven't had another night that bad.

Eric's Fireproof Shoes

One of the stops on the tour had a day off near a professional car racing team. I don't remember what class of car, I just remember Eric coming to the gig with all his swag. One of the items he got was a pair of fire proof shoes like the drivers wear. He thought these would be cool to wear these for the gig, as KISS is so well known for their pyro and fire. So wear them he did.

The show started as normal, but after the first song Eric complained that his right kick drum pedal didn't feel right; I had to change it out for a spare. To do this while he played I had to crawl around him quickly loosen the set screws, remove the old pedal, attach the new pedal, tighten the screws on that, and crawl out of there, which I did. After I changed his right pedal things still didn't feel right. He told me that the left pedal needed to be changed out and another spare had to be put in its place. This was just as much a pain in the ass as the first one, but I did it, that was my job.

By now I was beginning to suspect that there was nothing wrong with the pedals at all, but Eric is such a precision player I knew something had to be wrong. When he told me things still didn't feel right I looked at him and told him it must be those brand new fire proof shoes you've got on. He agreed, which left only one course of action. I had to leave the stage, run to his dressing room and grab the shoes he normally wore, which I did.

When I got back to the drum riser I had a feeling how this next part was going to go. A KISS concert is a high energy, well planned out show. There was no way the band was going to stop playing and wait for Eric to change his shoes. "Ladies and Gentlemen, KISS would like to announce a five minute intermission while our drummer deals with a wardrobe malfunction". That was never going to happen. The whole point was to take care of these types of problems without affecting show quality.

Well, that left me one choice; yes I had to change his shoes for him while he played. First I had to change one, then the other, not too tight, tie a double knot so it won't come out. Having done that, suddenly all was right with the kick drum pedals, and the show continued on. Here's where I give Eric a little credit, there is no way anybody would have heard anything in his playing that would let them know things were anything other than normal up there, he literally didn't miss a beat. With all the pit crew style shenanigans we were having, it would have been easy to screw up a song, but he was a pro.

If memory serves, that was the only appearance his fire proof shoes ever made at a gig I was on, at least as far as I can remember.

Alive 3

Part of the way into the tour there were rumblings that the band might be recording Alive 3, their third live concert album. As things progressed this became a reality. We would we recording three shows in the mid-west and possibly record at sound check. As a kid I spent hours reading the liner notes on their first two live albums, I could tell you who each crew member was, so it was cool to be involved with this record. There would be some video recording as well, so everything had to look good. Initially the band wanted me in some sort of a black hood so you couldn't see me, as I was so prominent on Eric's drum riser. Our production manager Tim talked them out of it, pointing out that someone in a hood would be more obvious than a regular crew guy that people are used to seeing.

Since there would be recordings from three shows to work with if there was a problem one night, we would be OK. The band had Eddie Kramer on site, as he would be producing this record. When he arrived I didn't know him by face, although I have always been a fan of his work. At the gig a guy with no laminate came on stage before sound check and started looking around, checking things out. I figured he was someone that didn't belong on stage so I asked him if I could help him, he said no and left. A little while later he was back on stage poking around so I told him to get the hell off the stage, which he did. It was Eddie Kramer, I had no idea. The shows all went fine and I think that the band got what they were looking for. It wasn't long after that the tour was over. There wasn't any talk about another tour or record, so for now I was on hold with KISS.

Africa Fete

After the Revenge tour I decided to spend a little more time at home. KISS and Alice were both going through a quiet period, so I thought this might be a good time to try something new. I spent most of the year in a variety of business pursuits outside of music. The only music work I did was for Steve Botting. He had called me and asked if I wanted to drive the Gipsy Kings gear from New York into Canada. It was an easy gig, I saw the show, they loaded the truck and I was on my way to Toronto for a show the next day. I got through customs and went to the gig, unloaded, crashed at the hotel for a couple of hours, and took the truck home. It was little adventure that I was well paid for.

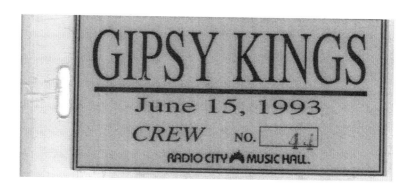

My Gipsy Kings laminate

Later in the year Steve called to see if I was interested in doing a short little tour in the States with bands from Africa and Haiti. It sounded intriguing, so I ended up doing it. There were four bands on the bill, and their crew spoke mostly French. I was there to run the stage; we had four bands sound checking and four bands doing a show. Sometimes I didn't leave the stage for eight hours; the sound checks would run right up until show time.

The lineup consisted of artists who were all very big in areas all over the world, but had yet to break into the market in the U.S. The bands and artists on this tour were Baaba Maal, Anjelique Kidjo, Ismail Lo and Boukman Eksperyans. When I took this tour I had never heard of any of them, but on the tour I got to know and enjoy all their music. There is so much good music around the world that you just never get the opportunity to hear, after this tour I made a habit of checking out all types of music, I still do.

Baaba Maal had a very distinctive voice, and he had a good sized band with him. These guys were serious players. One of the guys played what I later learned was called a "Talking Drum". The drum shell is shaped like an hourglass and the top and bottom skins are tied together so that when you squeeze you can change the pitch of the drum. Baaba had one segment of the show where he would sing something and his talking drum player would make his drum say it back. They would go back and forth like this, it was pretty impressive. A year later I was in a theater in L.A. for the premiere of "The Lion King" and when the movie started I instantly recognized that voice, it was Baaba Maal. I guess the Disney people must have heard of him.

Also on the bill was Anjelique Kidjo, another incredible performer. She managed to weave African drums and beats into her high energy dance music. Anjelique had a good band also, but it was obvious that she was in charge. She would tear that stage up every night, she was all over the place, and she had moves. She was something else to watch.

Ismael Lo was a guitar player and singer. His shows were a little more laid back and his songs had a little more heart and soul. There were so many performers and the days were so hectic that I rarely got to sit and talk to anyone, but one day I got to talk to Ismael before he went on. I had just fixed his guitar and when he thanked me he told me that when he agreed to come to the U.S. that he didn't know what to expect, I assumed he meant racial issues. He said that he was glad that we were on the crew and that he was happy that he came. All I said to him was that the only thing that mattered was the music, and he agreed, and with that we shook hands. Color never came into it, and I was glad for that too.

And finally, there was Boukman Eksperyans, who were from Haiti. They were almost all related, and I can't remember how many people were on stage, but you would see the whole family, Grandpa all the way down to a four year old grandchild, all playing drums and singing. There were all sorts of drums, some I had never seen before. Again, it was a very impressive and unique thing to see. I still have CD's from all these groups and once in a while I'll put them on.

A lot of these groups had side men, paid musicians in their band. They would be at the gigs a little more and even through the language barrier I got to know a lot of them. These guys appreciated anything you did for them. If you got them a set of guitar strings it was a big deal, because where they came from they were hard to get. When Africa Fete was over, I was glad that I had done it.

I forgot to mention that Ralph came out with me on this tour, he was the lighting guy. Ralph had worked for Steve in the past, so we both went out. Originally I was also going to drive the truck, but when we realized how long my day was on stage it was impossible. Ralph ended up helping out until they brought out another crew guy to drive.

Prior to the tour Steve Botting had told me that the tour producer wanted to have actual huts to sell merchandise out of, but they couldn't find anyone to build them. Ralph and his family were in construction, so they ended up with the gig, we built them in Ralph's parent's driveway. It was fun, and easy money. I was always glad for any chance to go to Ralph's parent's house. They are both great people and his Mom always fed us really well. I had a few friends whose parents always made me feel welcome and Mr. and Mrs. Ferreri were always the first to invite you in for a meal or just to hang out. It was sort of like having parents for a couple of hours.

Meat Loaf

Early in '94 I got a call from John Miceli, an old friend from the club days. He had gotten the gig as Meat Loafs drummer as was getting ready to play Madison Square Garden, definitely a big gig. The problem was that his drum tech had an emergency and had to go home for a couple of days; John needed me to tech the Garden show and also Stabler Arena in Pennsylvania. I was happy to do it, I hadn't seen a show on this tour yet, and new gigs are always fun.

I took the train into Manhattan the morning of the gig. I made my way to the production office to let them know who I was. The stage manager got me a laminate and showed me where my gear was, and I got to work. I had done this a thousand times before, so to me it was just another day. John arrived for sound check, we tweaked the drums a little bit, and we were ready. John didn't need much during the show so I didn't have a lot of cues to worry about.

The show started fine and went smoothly right up until intermission. They always had a short break during the show, Meat had a quick change room behind the stage, I guess he would towel off or change and catch his breath. On his way to the quick change he came over behind the drum riser to find me. He came right up to me, asked me my name, shook my hand and thanked me for helping out. I've always thought that was a really cool thing to do. I've always respected him for that. The rest of the show went great; we loaded out and headed out to Pennsylvania.

The show at Stabler Arena was just like the Garden, all went fine, and it was nice going out on tour for three days. After the show we all drove to the airport in New York, the band and crew got a hotel there as they were flying the next day. I got a ride to the train station and took the Long Island Rail Road home. I didn't get all that far, it had started to snow and the storm had turned into a blizzard. The railroad had started to cancel trains and close stations. I train hopped and was able to get to a town called Patchogue, about thirty miles from where I lived.

Patchogue was the last stop, everyone was kicked off, and we were on our own. I didn't have a cell phone so I set out walking in the blizzard to find a pay phone and a cab home. There were no cabs and all the stores were closed, this blizzard had gotten pretty bad. I was able to find a Laundromat that was open, I went inside to get warm and use the phone. By now I knew I had two choices, sleep at the Laundromat, or ask my fiancée Monica to come get me in the snowstorm. I didn't want her driving in the bad weather, but it did make the most sense. I think she told me she averaged between fifteen and twenty miles an hour. I feasted on soup and coffee from the vending machine while I waited.

That's how rock and roll is, one day you're playing Madison Square Garden at the top of your game, and two days later you're a homeless hobo begging for a ride and eating soup out of the Laundromat machine. That's what I love about it, it's like a dark alley, no matter how prepared you think you are, you never know what's waiting for you up ahead in the darkness.

Open Skyz

After a year of not touring I realized where my heart was and set about looking for work. When you are out of the touring business for even a little while, people tend to lose your number. So I had to beat the bushes a little to find work. KISS, Alice Cooper and Deborah Gibson were all not touring at this time, so I had to find a new gig.

Todd Confessore called me and told me that friends of ours, a band called Open Skyz, were heading out on a club tour opening for a band called Mr. Big. They wanted me on the crew, which Todd and my friend Vinnie Kowalski were already on. I had never done a real club tour; the one with KISS could hardly count. I had also never worked for a support act before, which was no big deal but it did mean I would have to change the way I worked. I was used to setting up my gear with plenty of time to trouble shoot, as a crew guy on a support act I would usually have little or no time to set up and trouble shoot. It was just a different mind set. But I took the gig, I needed to work again.

I had known most of the Open Skyz band from when they were in a band called Valentine; I had done some gigs around Long Island with them occasionally. We started the tour in Harrisburg, Pennsylvania at a club called Metropolis. There we were greeted by the Mr. Big crew and were brought into the kitchen / production office to meet Butch, the production manager for Mr. Big. He introduced himself and immediately started talking to us like we were idiots. He assumed we had never toured before, so I guess he dumbed down his welcome speech. I'll never forget when he explained to us what a tour laminate was and how it was important that we not lose ours. I remember walking out to the club thinking that this was going to be a long two months.

We waited for Mr. Big to get done with sound check, and when they did we had our stage set up and ready to sound check in about twenty minutes. We were all very experienced and I think that the Mr. Big crew was a bit surprised. After Open Skyz played their set we had the stage cleared in less than ten minutes and was packed up shortly thereafter. Todd was called into the kitchen / production office later that night by Butch, who asked him, "Did you forget to tell me something?" Todd played it cool and asked what he was talking about, and Butch said something about our crew being more experienced than he thought. Todd looked at him and said, "Oh yeah, Vinnie and I have been out with Dream Theater, Kenny just got home from working for KISS" and on he went. I think Butch felt a little smaller after that.

The tour rolled on just fine, we were a group of good friends riding around doing shows, and it doesn't get any better than that. I got to see a lot of clubs I'd never been to before. Working for the support act had its advantages, since we were done so early, I got to go out in the club and watch Mr. Big, or just hang out. Since it was obvious I was with the tour, people were always quick to buy me a drink. The life of a support act tech wasn't as bad as I had thought. You set up later, play first and you're done early. I actually kind of liked it.

We got to play cool clubs like Tipitinas in New Orleans. We also got to go to The Anchor Bar in Buffalo, New York, where chicken wings were first made popular. The late load in schedule made for a relaxing tour, even though we were playing clubs in the winter.

The last gig was going to be a radio promo show called "The Blaze Fest". There were a lot of cool bands on the bill, and KISS was headling the show. Originally I had talked to Eric about doing the show as his tech also and he agreed, we tried to make it happen. But I couldn't be there in time for load in, so it wasn't going to work out. Eric did hold my job open for me though, he had a friend drum tech for him so that when KISS played more steadily I would still have my job. I have always appreciated that. Eric was one of the top drummers out there and there were a lot of good drum techs that wanted the gig, but he held it for me.

Anyway, we played the gig but rather than stay overnight, Vinnie and I decided to head straight home. The next day was Easter and we both wanted to be with our families. We drove the truck full of our gear all night and part of the day to get back to New York, and we made it home for the holiday. Although there was the time I was driving down the interstate and Vinnie waved at a cop in the next lane. Thirty seconds later I saw the flashing lights, we were getting pulled over. The cop was yelling about us being in the wrong lane, which we weren't. I just think that Vinnie pissed him off. Thanks Vin.

STP

After the Open Skyz tour there was a little club work, but I still needed to find a real gig. I had talked to Steve Botting and he had two or three small tours all lined up for the summer. He hired me for his crew and I was just glad to have something. My fiancée Monica had started to make plans for our wedding, so we picked a date when I would be home, now that I had a schedule.

A couple of days later the phone rang and it was Dan Stevenson, my production manager from the Alice Cooper tours. He was in Florida with a band called Stone Temple Pilots and he wanted me to come to rehearsals and do the tour. And he wanted me then, right then, that day. I told him I couldn't do it because of my prior commitment, my wedding, and business at home. I thanked him and hung up the phone. I told Monica about it and while I was still telling the story the phone rang, it was Dan again. All I heard on the phone was"We'll fly you home for your wedding, you can start with us tomorrow, and we'll pay you this much". Before I could even think I told him yes. I hung up the phone, told Monica, and started looking for the first STP cd; I knew I had it somewhere although I hadn't listened to it yet. I started packing and taking care of wedding plans, I had two hours to go pick out a tuxedo. I took care of all my business, called Steve Botting to tell him I took another gig, and the next day I was off to Florida, I wouldn't see Monica again for two months, for the wedding. That's how it goes sometime; it's not uncommon to get a phone call asking you to get on a plane that day. If a tour needs someone, they usually need them right away.

I flew into Miami and went straight to rehearsals, which were being done at a place called Comtel, basically a big soundstage facility. What I didn't know until I got there was that I was supposed to be replacing the current guitar tech, and he didn't know. The band were on a bigger stage than they had been in the past, and their one guitar tech couldn't be there for both the guitar and bass players as they were on opposite sides of the stage. The band was taking a big step up and this was just part of the growing process. I had to be in stealth mode as I walked around Comtel checking everything out. I didn't know anyone except Dan and he was working in the production office. When the band finally arrived they headed for the office to see what the status of the guitar tech situation was. It turned out that they guy they had, Eric, was an old friend and they didn't want to fire him, even though they felt they had to.

I'll never forget the first thing that Dean, the guitar player, said to me when I met him in the production office that day. He looked me right in the eye and said "I didn't want you coming out here". Here we go I thought, I'll be home by tomorrow. We talked about what was going wrong with the tech situation and it didn't take me long to figure out that they just hadn't realized yet that they needed two guitar techs. On their first tour they started out as a new band playing anywhere with a minimal crew. In that time they had earned a Grammy, gone multi platinum, and had become an important band in the music scene. This was their graduation to the big time. When I talked to them about having two guitar techs they seemed to think that might be the answer to the problem. They wanted to go back out to the stage and run the whole show with both of us, and see how it felt. I had to tell them that I didn't know any of their songs yet, so it might be a little rough, but we ran the show anyway and all went well. Dan told me later that they were happy with the new arrangement and that we would keep Eric on as bass tech. The first day was done, now I just had to learn the songs, the gear, all my cues, and a hundred other things.

While the rest of the crew went out that night I stayed in and listened to the new cd, and I also spent some time sewing. There was a song where Dean needed three guitar slides with him, as he would use one, discard it, play chords and need another one. A guitar slide is a metal tube that fits over your finger so you can slide it over the strings. Their song "Big Empty" was the one that needed the slide; it was a big hit and a high point of the show. I sewed up a prototype that night and the next day Dean used it and liked it. We never made another, he always used the prototype I made, and when I saw him play with his band Army of Anyone a year or two ago, he still had it.

Rehearsals continued to go well. I learned the music and Dean and I got a certain rhythm to the guitar changes. I did bang him in the head once or twice taking the guitar off him too fast; he wasn't used to that kind of attention and I caught him off guard. I also set about getting road cases that were needed and making sure that we were ready equipment wise, to do this tour.

After rehearsals at Comtel we loaded out and loaded into the Knight Center in Miami for full rehearsals. The Knight Center was the first venue of the tour so this was a good opportunity to try out the full show.

The set that the guys had was beautiful, they had huge lava lamps on either side of the stage, and they had to be fifteen to twenty feet high. Where the liquid would normally be in a lava lamp, they had projection screens with projectors inside. They could make these things look like real lava lamps, or anything else. The entire back of the stage had beautiful purple drapes; the name of the new cd was "Purple". For the acoustic part of the show there was a whole living room set that was brought out on stage, also a very cool look. There was also a front curtain that would open to reveal the band.

The rehearsals at the Knight Center went really well and the first show also ran smoothly. It was a big relief to get the first show out of the way, now the tour could really start. The next show was in Tampa and that show went off without a problem. After Tampa we were heading to Orlando to play the Edge Concert Field, an outdoor show. After set up and sound check there was a threat of rain and it wasn't long before it hit, and it hit pretty hard. The band wanted to play anyway; I was called into production to see if this was feasible. In my opinion it wasn't safe for the band to be out there, and I told them. This band didn't like wireless systems on their guitars, they preferred the old school way, plugging in with a wire. It did sound better, but it also made the possibility of electrocution a very real threat. When you use wireless the rain may damage your gear, but you're relatively safe.

The band didn't want to cancel and there was a fear that there might be a riot. On their last tour playing with other bands there had been a riot and the stage was overrun, they hadn't forgotten it. So provisions were made for the announcement, most of the crew left on a tour bus and the band got out of there as well. The plan was for the crew to come back and pack up after the threat of a riot was over. I stayed behind to pack up my guitars and gear, I didn't care if there was a riot or not, I wasn't losing any gear today. While I was packing up I saw a horrible sight off the back of the stage, a purple river. The rain had taken a lot of the dye off those beautiful drapes and there was purple everywhere.

After a while the crew came back, there hadn't been any trouble at the gig after all. The gear was put into the trucks and we headed for New Orleans as fast as we could. Arrangements had been made to get into the arena as soon as we got there, so the drapes could be hung and dried, and so that all the other gear could also be dried out.

In New Orleans we were able to get the gear dried out, but the curtains never looked the same. By now the tour was up and running, I think the shows were sold out just about everywhere. When the record came out it went to number one, and it spawned a lot of top ten hits. The band had initially booked only ten weeks in the States and after a break, five weeks in Europe. As well as their record did, I think they could have toured for two years. The shows looked and sounded good; when the band was having a good night they were one of the best bands I had ever seen.

We hammered it out through most of the summer. Early in August it was getting close to my fly out date for my wedding. For some reason there were no guitar techs available, I couldn't find anyone. I was starting to get desperate and started calling everyone I knew to put the word out. Finally, Louie Appel came up with someone, a guy named Jim. Jim flew out sight unseen, I walked him through the gear and he watched me do a show. After that he took over for a few days. He ended up doing a couple of shows and a video, the band had decided to do one on a day off, so Jim was there for it. I got back after my brief break and Jim stayed to watch a show from out front before he left. The tour was back into high gear for me.

A couple of days after I returned to the tour we broke away from the STP shows and headed up to Toronto to open for the Rolling Stones. This was a big deal and a good opportunity for the band to play in front of a large audience. My tour itinerary lists the capacity at Exhibition Stadium where we played, at 53,116. Like I said this was going to be a big crowd. We rolled into the stadium and were immediately greeted by Charlie Hernandez, my former KISS production manager. He was part of the production team for the Stones, and he introduced us around so we could start getting ready.

The first thing that impressed us was the size of the stage; it was easily one of the biggest I had been on. Since the STP guys didn't use wireless I could only be about thirty feet away from the band, which meant that I was working right on stage during the show, with no place to hide. When the Stones were done with the stage we got started setting up and it was really obvious that our set up was like a postage stamp on that stage. We had to keep the spacing of the guitar amps and monitors the same as our normal show, so the band couldn't spread out. And since the guys were on guitar cables instead of wireless, they couldn't use half that real estate to run around.

The first night went really well and it was cool getting to see the Stones. A few of us stuck around to watch the show. The only problem was, with as big a crowd as there was at the stadium, they couldn't get the busses out, the crew all had to make their way back to the hotel. I eventually got a cab, but only by waving a fifty dollar bill, which I never did give the cabby. When I got to the hotel I paid him and tipped him, but he was grumbling about the fifty, I just took off for the hotel.

We got to the stadium for the second show, and we were told that the weather forecast was for rain. Charlie and his people wanted to make sure we had a rain plan, which I knew we didn't. When asked, the band guys just said that if it rained, they wouldn't play. In response, the Stones production people made it clear that that was not an option. Charlie had one of the guitar techs, Pierre, set us up with some of their spare wireless units. I set mine up with Dean's guitar rig and you could hear the difference. I got it to sound as good as I could and just hoped for the best. We got lucky, we were able to do the whole show without the wireless system, and it was another good night.

I stayed on to watch the Stones again and they were something else to see. They're legends, there's nothing else out there like them. The stage was massive, the lights were incredible, and the stage set was amazing. They were the culmination of years of experience, and the money and talent to do whatever they wanted. Those have been the only times I have seen the Stones live, but I do hope to again. After that second show it was time to go. With our truck loaded and the shows over we headed out for the next stop on the STP Purple tour.

Back on the Purple Tour

We didn't really have enough security for these shows; I don't think anyone could have predicted the mayhem we would see night after night. There were sections of the show where we could no longer do guitar changes because of the amount of stage jumpers during certain songs. I was out there grabbing kids as much as I was tuning guitars. And toward the end of the show when the band would play "Sex Type Thing" it got really crazy. Anybody that had been thinking about heading on stage knew that this was their last chance, so this was when it was hard to keep up with the amount of kids coming over the barricade. Some nights the local security just gave up and we were on our own.

The tour started to head over to the east coast, closer to my home, so my wife was able to start coming to shows. She really liked the band so she came out when she could. There was a full length concert video shot on this leg of the tour, in Massachusetts I think, but I don't know whatever happened to it. To this day I have never seen it. That was one thing about these guys, if they didn't like how something came out, they wouldn't release it. I don't know if that's the case here, but hopefully one day I'll get to check that show out myself.

The tour wound down the east coast and ended in Florida. This had actually been a tough tour for me and I was glad it was over. I had had a few bad nights myself, gear problems etc. And since the rest of the crew had been with the band practically since day one, I never really fit in with them. Which is OK, you don't click with everyone and it is just a job. It would be a few weeks before the band headed to Europe, we just had to do an MTV thing in New York and then I could go home. I just assumed that was my last STP gig and went on my way. I wasn't home more than a few days before I started getting phone calls from the guys about preparations for the Europe tour. Nobody was more surprised than me, I figured they would get someone else, somebody from Los Angeles, but no, I was going.

The back of my STP tour laminate

Purple in Europe

We started the European leg of the Purple tour mid October of '94. As before our rehearsals were at the first gig, which was in Dublin, Ireland. STP was not as big outside the U.S., so we were playing much smaller venues. This first venue was the SFX Centre, which was a fourteen hundred seat theater. We had scaled down for this leg and had a much smaller crew. After touring the States in larger buildings it was odd to see the band crammed onto these smaller stages. One other issue we had was power, our amps ran on one hundred and ten volts, and all of Europe runs on two hundred and forty, so we would have to use step down transformers. For a lot of gear this wouldn't be a big deal, but tube guitar amps can be fussy with power. I spent the whole tour pulling power from different places, isolating my power from other equipment to get rid of buzzes. Also power wasn't consistent and we had no provision for this. There is equipment out there that can regulate your power and avoid these problems, but we weren't carrying any. At some of the venues my power would start to dip down during the show, as more current was being used. This wreaks havoc with how a guitar amp sounds, and there are some electronics that just shut down if the voltage gets too low. The power issues kept me busy, but they never caused any major show problems.

We got through the rehearsals and the first show, and now we would be heading over to Scotland for our next show at The Barrowlands, a nineteen hundred seat venue. It is also known as The Glasgow Barrowland Ballroom. The gig was what looked like an old dance hall that was up several flights of really wide steps, like you see in old movies. The guys on the crew there are some of the toughest stagehands I have ever met. They would run these cases up the stairs, like I had seen the crew at the Ritz in New York do years before. And if one of them got hurt, the other guys would point and laugh at him. When they were done loading in the equipment they would kick a ball around the venue, it was an all out no holds barred game of soccer / football, where they were kicking the crap out of each other. I have been to the Barrowlands many times and they have never missed a game. The gig went fine and now we were off to Wolverhampton, and then London to play Brixton Academy, where we would also end the tour in about five weeks. We played a few more shows in the U.K. before heading out to Belgium. After Belgium we went through Germany, Holland, Norway, Sweden and Denmark, before heading back to Germany. All the gigs were about the same size, anywhere from fifteen hundred to three thousand.

When we were in Germany I heard one of the funniest things I have ever heard from a local crew guy. Some of our guys were smoking cigarettes in a building where it wasn't allowed. The stage hands didn't like this so they started yelling "Rauchen Verboten" or something like that; I guess it meant smoking forbidden. Our guys didn't care so they started trading insults with the German crew. Finally, this old withered man comes over; he was older than dirt, and said to one of our guys in English with a heavy German accent, "I shot your father in the war". As he pointed his gnarled index finger and repeated his insult, our guys were stunned; they had no comeback for that. They put out their cigarettes and walked away.

Now it was on to France, Switzerland, Italy, and Spain for pretty much more of the same. They band went over well every night; I thought they were making good progress in the European market.

One of the gigs that really stands out was Aqualung in Madrid, Spain. The way I remember it, it was more like a big club, a two thousand seat club. The place was packed to the rafters, and these kids were going crazy. With so many people in there it got incredibly hot, especially on stage under the lights. During the show the roof started leaking and fried one of our power supplies, a really hokey unit provided locally. I had to do some messing around with live two hundred and forty volts to get it back up and running, which went fine. After the show during load out a few of us saw that it hadn't been raining outside at all. The rain in the building was all the people's sweat evaporating and rising to the ceiling, collecting, and raining down. I have never seen anything like that before or since.

Another memory of that night involved one of Dean's cherished guitars. Toward the end of the set he liked to take off his guitar and throw it to me, which I always caught, until tonight. He threw, the lights on stage went out, and I missed. His guitar landed and the neck snapped off. He was heartbroken and I felt like crap. You can see a picture of him with the broken guitar in the liner notes on one of their CDs.

Anyway, it was back to Brixton Academy where the band stopped mid show to have a best drummer contest. Guys from STP, the crew and other bands all took a turn, I forget who won. After that the show continued as normal. The show ended, the lights came up and the Purple tour was over.

A laminate from a European festival, it says it all

The Ladder Up (And Down)

There are different levels of bands in the business, and there are crew guys that work their way either up or down the levels, depending on how well their career is going.

Initially most guys start out with a local band playing local bars. The hope is to get a spot opening for someone bigger, and meeting other crew guys so you can get your name out. Either a band you work for would be able to do a club tour or open for a national act on tour. The idea is to get on the road and work your way up. Once you're on a crew, you meet other crew guys that can recommend you, and when there's an opening, hope that your skills are up to the challenge. With luck you might be in the right place, at the right time, with the right skills when a bigger band needs someone. As I said earlier, when there is an opening it usually has to be filled immediately, and if you're there, it might be your time.

The idea is to work for a band that plays arenas regularly, these gigs are the steadiest and pay the best. Back in the day bands on this level were known to keep their guys on payroll year round, whether there were shows or not. That way they could count on you to always be there. There aren't a lot of bands doing that now, but the arena gigs are still what you want. And when you get to the arena level the idea is to stay there. Keep your shit together and do good work. Too many guys don't hold it together; they screw up their gig with too much partying and end up working their way back down the ladder. Believe me; you don't want to go from an arena band back to the clubs. It isn't pretty.

Dictionary:

Backline Crew: The crew that handle the bands amps, drums and instruments. The amp line and drums are known as the Backline.

Barricade: Structure built in front of the stage designed to prevent people from getting on stage.

Drum Riser: The elevated platform that the drum kit is set up on.

Gig: A show, a job.

Itinerary: Booklet given to you with all pertinent tour information; hotel and gig phone numbers, etc.

Laminate: The laminated pass worn by members of the touring party that signifies that they are part of the tour.

Road Case: Case specifically built for carrying delicate equipment on and off trucks and airplanes.

Set: A group of songs that the band plays.

Shed: An outdoor open air amphitheater.

Stage Left: The left hand part of the stage from your perspective when you face the audience.

Stage Right: The right hand part of the stage from your perspective when you face the audience.

Swag: Merchandise given to you for free, typically with a band or company's logo on it.

174

Back with KISS

January of '95 found me back in Los Angeles rehearsing with KISS. We would be doing shows in Japan and Australia, and it felt good to be among friends again. By now I was a regular part of the KISS crew, I didn't have to prove myself all over, and I could just do my gig. During rehearsals talking with the band, Gene asked what I had been doing, and I told him that I just finished guitar teching for Stone Temple Pilots. He responded by asking me if I meant drum teching, and I said no, that I had originally started out as a guitar tech, and that's what I was doing when Eric and I toured together on Alice Cooper. Initially I could tell he was surprised, but I remember noticing a look he gave me, like he was filing away that piece of info for later. I knew it then and I would be proven right in a couple of months.

Rehearsals went fine and before I knew it we were heading out to Japan, where KISS were still doing good business. We would be going to Osaka, Tokyo and a few other cities. And of course Udo Artists would be handling the tour. This was another paid vacation as far as I was concerned. I love Japan, I was back with KISS, and soon we would be heading to Australia. This was a good run. All the shows went great and the people from Udo Artists made us all feel right at home. Before I knew it I was on a plane heading to Australia.

Since KISS hadn't been to Australia in about fifteen years, this was a big deal. When we landed the airport was jammed with fans and the press. The band was led out a separate exit and the crew just headed out like normal. I was surprised when a guy I didn't know walked up to me and said "Hello Ken, how's it going?" I didn't know what was going on with him until he pulled out a tour book from the Revenge tour, which had my picture and name in it. All he wanted was an autograph, which I have never minded doing. I've never understood why anyone would want my autograph, but I'll always oblige.

The tour was handled by Frontier Touring, who was the big promoter down there. I was to find out that they were handling the concerts and also the conventions in Australia. On days when we didn't have an arena gig the band had KISS conventions of their own set up with all sorts of displays, and the band would play. I ended up setting up the display that had the drums Peter Criss played when he was with the band, and I teched for Eric as well. The conventions were different and the bands set was really laid back, a real departure from the arena shows we normally did.

Doing the conventions meant that the backline crew really didn't get any days off on this tour, but the conventions were a cool thing to check out. Occasionally I would find an old KISS collectible and haggle for it, sometimes I would be asked for autographs, or just get asked questions about working for the band. I have always enjoyed doing this, let's face it, it's those people buying tickets that paid for my house, in a way I work for them. Without them I wouldn't have done a lot of the cool things I've gotten to do. Thank you. The arena shows were all great and again, before I knew it I was on a plane home. There was talk of upcoming work, so I knew it wouldn't be long before I was back in the KISS camp.

Television

One of the ways I was able to keep busy between tours was by working in television. Throughout my career I had the good fortune of working for bands that appeared on late night or early morning programs. As a lot of these were shot where I lived, New York, and I made a point of getting to know the producers. If a band or artist were booked for a show and didn't have a crew, or couldn't bring their crew, often times I would get a call to come out.

Working on the David Letterman Show or Conan O'Brien was always a good time. I could take the train to Manhattan in the morning, load in, and hang out a bit. When the artist arrived I would make sure they had what they needed. Sound check would be in the late afternoon, and taping would start between five and six. Once the taping was over, load out was always quick, once the gear was packed the union guys would handle the rest of load out. I would take the train home and arrive in time to have dinner with my wife, and after dinner we would stay up and watch the show I had taped. While you're working the show you can't see what's going on out front, so it was always cool to watch the show later.

The morning shows were a little different. Often I would have to go in around midnight if the shoot was outdoors, or four or five in the morning if we were shooting in the studio. The early shows were good because I could take the train and get home before noon, I'd still have a lot of the day left.

Carly

In the spring of '95 I started working for Carly Simon, doing gigs around New York. These gigs were always low key and easy. There were two techs to do the gigs, sometimes it was only Carly and one or two band guys, sometimes the whole band. There were even gigs around New York where it was just Carly and a guitar. She had an equipment locker for her guitars and gear; we would go there the day before the gig, restring instruments and make sure all was well. Occasionally she needed a guitar at home so one of us would drop it off at her apartment. Gig days were easy, Carly and the band were old pros who knew what they needed. It never took long for sound check.

We did David Letterman with the whole band, which was more of a full days work. Bobby, the other tech, and I were working backstage tuning guitars when Dave was heading out to his desk on stage. He saw us working and made a point of coming over to say hello and ask how we were doing. Every time I've done the show Dave has always been really great.

We did a radio station promo gig up in Massachusetts where there was a non stop rotation of artists, and Carly was on the bill in the afternoon. Tom Jones was there and before she went on Carly asked him to come out and do "You're So Vain" with her. He did, and he was incredible. Tom is still one of the coolest people on the planet. After a few more gigs Carly was heading out on tour with Hall and Oates and the tour was using one crew, theirs, which I knew already. That was OK by me because by then I had confirmed the next Kiss tour, which would be starting soon.

KISS Conventions

I had gotten the call to do the KISS convention tour while still working for Carly Simon. For those of you that don't know, KISS conventions have been going on for years, but they have always been done by people other than the band. This convention would have displays of memorabilia from the bands personal collection, costumes from throughout the years, events through the day capped off with an acoustic performance by the band. After the live show the band would stay and sign autographs for as long as it took to make sure everyone got one.

This tour was going to be run by a very small crew, which brings me back to what I said earlier about Gene. The entire crew was all responsible to put up the displays, mannequins with costumes, the sound and lights, and band gear. But when it came time for the live show, I would be taking care of Eric and Gene, since Gene knew I could do guitars also. Mike Rush was taking care of Paul and Bruce. At each convention there was a tribute band that would do a KISS show, and often times I would help those guys out also.

For the most part the conventions were held in the ballroom of the hotel where we were staying. Since the days were long this was a plus, if you needed a break you could just head up to your room for a few. Load in was first thing in the morning, and we had to hustle to make the noon start time. We each had our own displays that we would set up first, we would often times set up the band gear after the convention started, we didn't need it until much later. I ended up with the displays of memorabilia, the magazine cover display, the displays with the old merchandise like the lunch boxes, etc. It was more time consuming to set up the mannequins with the costumes, so most of the crew would concentrate on those, and I would knock out all the displays that just needed to be built.

Once the displays were finished we would get the sound and lights set up by the stage area. Kevin Valentine was the sound engineer; we would work with him and get a sound check done. When the KISS equipment was ready we would help set up the tribute band. By now with everything ready, we would be able to grab lunch and kick back for a little while, there wasn't a whole lot for us to do until the tribute band started playing.

When the doors were first opened and the fans came in there was always a rush to see everything. Between the displays and the vendors there was a lot to go through, but after a couple of hours there was a definite lull in the excitement. We needed just a little something to keep things rolling through the afternoon. As a veteran of many a Star Trek convention, I knew what would work, I suggested to Tommy Thayer that we have a KISS trivia contest during the slow time. One of the guys would walk around the audience with a microphone and one of the guys on stage would ask prepared question. KISS fans pride themselves on knowing everything about the band, so there was never a lack of participants. Small prizes were given out and it did fill an empty spot in the day. A funny thing about that though, not long after the convention tour there was an article in one of the KISS magazines about one of the other crew guys, and he took credit for the trivia contest and my auction idea. I thought that was pretty crappy, but what can you do?

The auction idea I had was simple, auction off merchandise that we already sell, the difference being that the winner would get private face time with the band before they came out to play, so they could get it personally autographed. Two items were put up for auction and both went for an astronomical sum, a big success. As a thank you Tommy Thayer gave me a copy of the KISS book "KISSTORY", which was cool. Even though it did well, we didn't have any more auctions. I heard different reasons why, but nothing official.

The first U.S. convention was in Burbank, California on June 17. This was the first convention in America, so there was no way to know how it would go over. It turned out to be a great success, as did the entire tour. This was just what the fans wanted. It was at this first convention the original drummer; Peter Criss came down and actually sang with the band. The entire room went wild when he came out to play. I think that the fans really liked seeing KISS in the relaxed atmosphere of the convention, doing an acoustic set. Their normal arena shows are always so polished and fast paced, these convention shows let the fans see who the guys really were, at least a little bit.

The convention tour wound around the West Coast, and then we went through Vegas, Texas, Louisiana, Florida and all parts in between. The days were long but they were always interesting, you never knew what to expect from the fans. Some would come in costumes that they made themselves that looked just like the real thing.

We then headed up through the Midwest and into Canada. One thing about this tour though, there were weeks where we had three or four days off in a row, in a nice hotel. Normally that would be a good thing, but too much time off gives you too much time to get into trouble. There was a night out in Chicago when I went out drinking with the merchandise guy, his name was Fly. We ended up in and Irish pub hanging out with some tourists from Ireland. My family is originally from Ireland so this was the sort of place where I would usually end up. We were having a great time hanging out, talking and drinking with everyone. The whiskey and beer was flowing and before I knew it I had fallen off my bar stool. Fly picked me up and dusted me off, and I assured him I was OK. We ordered another round and about a minute later I fell off my bar stool again. That was it, I was cut off.

Fly hauled me out of the bar and got me into a cab, and he paid the cabbie extra to get me into the hotel. When we got to the hotel the cabbie hauled me out of the cab, I was a wreck by now, and heaved me into the hotel lobby. I didn't make it three steps before I was down again. The hotel staff was none too happy about this. I offered the bellman some cash to haul me up to my room in his luggage cart, but he said he couldn't. I explained that there were three choices here; he could make some money and haul me to my room, he could leave me there for all the hotel guests to see, or he could call the police which would cause a big scene that the hotel didn't need. Even in my drunken stupor I had figured this out. He took the fifty bucks and got me upstairs.

You would think that the story would end there, and I wish it did, but it doesn't. I had developed a hangover preventive/cure during my time on the road. I would lay in the shower with the tub stopper in. Most hotel stoppers have a pressure switch that prevents the tub from overflowing. I would lie in the tub and let it fill, but I would keep the shower running the whole time I was in there. I had been doing this for years and it always helped. Usually I would be in there fifteen minutes to a half hour. This particular evening I didn't wake up until about ten the next morning, I had been in there for eight hours. It was a wonder I didn't drown. My skin was so pruned up it hurt, and it stayed that way for about a day. I spent the rest of the time off in Chicago laying low and recovering.

By now we were hearing a lot of rumors that started when Peter sang with the band. There was talk that the original members might play together, but these were rumors, nothing official from the band. Finally word came down that the band would be taping MTV's Unplugged after the tour. But nothing was said about Ace and Peter.

One of the things that came about from the producers of Unplugged was that Gene needed to play an acoustic bass. Although the band had been playing an acoustic set on tour, Gene had been using an electric bass through a small amp. So my job was to round him up an acoustic bass that would have a little punch to it, acoustic or not this was still Gene Simmons. Originally Gene wanted to try acoustics on the road through his amp. When I told him I thought it was a bad idea because they would tend to feed back and be a pain in the ass through the amp, he asked what I wanted to do. I told him that since we had rehearsal days at S.I.R. studios, it would be better if I got a bunch of basses to try, and just hammer it out. I knew when we found the right bass we would know it. This is why I got along well with Gene, he asked me one question, "Can you make that happen?" and I gave him a one word answer, yes. He gave me a one word response, "Done"

On the first day at S.I.R. there were a ton of basses to try, some guy even had a hand made one that he built himself that he wanted to give Gene. We tried all the basses once, and then went back to the obvious choice, a Kramer acoustic bass that had balls. It definitely stood out. I knew it wouldn't take long, we both knew what we were looking for. Now I just had to round up a second one, for a spare.

I sort of jumped ahead there, let me wrap up the convention tour first, and then get to the taping. After Canada we had our last conventions in Boston, New York City, and Pittsburgh. The Boston convention was held in the hotel ballroom, but for NYC we went to the Roseland Ballroom, a facility better equipped for a New York KISS crowd. We had more room to work with, and I was able to take over the bottom level with my displays, while the costumed mannequins were all on the main level. Spreading out like this helped keep the crowd moving. Andy Richter from the Conan O'Brien show was there and filmed a few segments. In a couple of days the band were scheduled to appear on Conan's show, playing unplugged as they had all summer. The New York convention went really well and so did Pittsburgh. After a little get together in one of the hotel suites, it was time to get packed, I was flying home for the days off, before we did Conan and another taping.

184

KISS Unplugged Shoot

The Unplugged shoot was going to be a really big deal; there was no telling what this could lead to (although we know now). KISS unplugged was one thing, but the wheels were in motion to bring Ace and Peter in for this, which was enormous. I was glad to be involved with this shoot, although I was pretty busy for this one. Not only was I teching for Gene and Eric, I would also be taking care of Peter, who I really didn't know at all.

For rehearsals I knew Eric would be OK. I got his drums ready first so he could warm up while Gene and I went through basses. Peter wouldn't be arriving until later, so I knew I had time to deal with him after Gene. Once Gene was dialed in I was able to work on Peters drums and get ready for when he arrived, which could be at any moment. After that it was pretty much auto pilot. The band started rehearsing and they sounded great. They were going through songs and working things out. Peter and Ace arrived later and they also got dialed in pretty quickly. The rest of the time at S.I.R. was standing by in case the guys needed something. We loaded out when the guys were done rehearsing, and loaded in for the shoot.

The studio where we would be working looked great, there was a big cloth replica of a KISS album cover on the floor, the whole set and lights looked great. We got the band gear set up and the guys ran through some songs. There was a little confusion as to who would get there when, so some of the guys didn't make it right away, but it all came together in the end. The show started with the current line up of KISS, but

185

you could see another drum kit up there under a cover, so it wasn't hard to figure out. The shoot was going fine and the audience loved it, but when Peter and Ace came out the place went wild. It was one of those magic moments that you hear about. Having the whole band play together was exactly what the audience was waiting for, and they got it.

On my end things went really well, there were no gear problems. Gene's bass stayed in tune and sounded great, both drum kits were fine. All I really needed to do was make sure the guys had towels and cold drinks, the rest of the gig took care of itself. At the end of the show we packed up the gear and headed home. This was the last gig I had with KISS until next year. In a few days I was heading down to South America with Alice Cooper for a few weeks, and as soon as I got home I would be starting with Ritchie Blackmore's Rainbow for a tour of Europe and Japan. I was actually booked for the rest of the year.

A few months later when the video came out, I was disappointed to see that some of the crew had been omitted from the credits. I had done a lot on this gig and I wanted it to count for something. I was glad that when the CD came out they included the rest of us.

South America with the Coop

A few days after I finished the KISS shows I was booked to go to South America with Alice. I hadn't done anything with the Cooper camp since the end of '91, so it was good to see some of the old faces again. Ralph was on this gig also, he was doing lights for Alice now, not drums. We were heading down to Sao Paolo, Brazil for about ten days of pre- production and rehearsals before we did any shows. I would be working for Stef and Derek again; I had worked for them on the '91 tour. The band also consisted of Paul Taylor, Greg Smith and on drums, Jimmy DeGrasso. My old friend Kevin "Batty" Walsh was the stage right tech and rounding out the backline crew was a new guy to the Cooper camp, Jeff "J Mann" Mann.

It was good to see everyone again; we all picked up right where we had left off. Initially Batty and I conspired to torture the new drum tech as we had tortured Ralph years before, but old habits die hard and we ended up picking on Ralph just like we had always done. Only now Ralph had a brand new guy to contend with. He didn't mind Batty and I so much, but when J Mann would give him crap he would actually get really pissed off, which just added more fuel for the fire for us. We all loved Ralph, but when it came to giving him grief, we couldn't help ourselves.

A lot of the other production crew were people we hadn't worked with, so the four of us sort of formed a core group, we hung out together, we drank (way too much) together, worked and ate together. Since all these rehearsals were like a day job and our gear stayed set up, we were able to go out all the time and

187

have a lot of fun. You would think we would have tried to see the sights of Brazil and check out the night life, but we didn't. Right across from our hotel on the beach there were these little stands that sold ice cold beer for almost no money. They had little plastic tables and chairs set out, and we ended up there almost every night. Getting drunk, being stupid. Other people would stop by and hang, and occasionally we would see a band guy or two, but mostly it was Ralph, J Mann, Batty and me. There was one night when Batty went down the steps to the beach to relieve himself by the sea wall. He heard something and looked up, and there right over his head was a steady stream from someone else relieving themselves from the sidewalk. He came back up to where we were drinking laughing so hard he turned red. Of course he accused me; he had known me a long time. I bought the next round and all was well.

There was another night when a few of the production crew were hanging with us, and a local guy came around with what he was trying to pass off as a girl, I had my doubts. One of the guys did a little half-assed translating and he figured out that the price tag was eighty dollars. All I could hear him say was "Eighty bucks, let's go!" and off he went across the street to our hotel. We spent the entire time he was gone making fun of him, so when he came walking back a half hour later with his arm around her like the conquering hero, we all burst out in laughter. Slowly he took his arm off her and started to distance himself. After a minute he was trying to claim he hadn't done anything, but there was no way anyone was going to believe him. Batty, Ralph, J Mann and I spent the rest of the trip torturing him over that one.

I know we played a few gigs on this tour, but most of the stories and my memories are from when we weren't working. The first show is South America was the Monsters of Rock festival, which was at the Pacaembu Stadium right in Sao Paolo. They love rock in South America and are some of the best audiences in the world. The load in and sound check went as normal, no surprise there. There were a few bands on before Alice, and you could tell that this was going to be a wild night. Before Alice went on the backline crew needed to test the guitar rigs at full volume to make sure everything was OK. Most bands don't like you to play their songs, so Batty and I were doing other peoples riffs. Batty started playing the Megadeth song "Symphony of Destruction" and the audience went crazy. I started playing the STP song "Vasoline" and the crowd went equally crazy. I always knew those guys could be big around the world. Years later I told them about the audience reaction and they were blown away.

The lights went down, Alice and the band took the stage, and kicked ass the whole night. This was a great audience for the Coop, and it was clear that he still had it. The show went great, so after the last note it was time for load out, then head back to the hotel for one last night out before heading to Rio de Janeiro for the next show. All in all we ended up playing the gigs in Brazil, we played Santiago, Chile and we ended the tour in Buenos Aires, Argentina. We had done gigs with Ozzy, Megadeth and a lot of other metal bands. The shows were fun and it had been great to work with the old crew again. Now there was some talk of the Coop working more, and I was glad to hear it.

Ritchie Blackmore's Rainbow

Before leaving for South America I had already been offered the Rainbow tour, which would start as soon as I got back. It was nice to have my next job locked in, and this tour would keep me working for most of the year. I have always been a Deep Purple and Rainbow fan, so I was glad to have this gig. John O'Reilly was playing drums and he was the one to initially contact me. I had done gigs around the bars with John for years. Originally I think I was going to tech for him and Greg Smith, who was playing bass. In the interim it was decided that John wasn't doing the tour, Chuck Burgi was, and I would be keyboard teching only. I had never done a tour where I did keyboards only; usually I was handling guitars also, so this made for an easier gig than I was used to.

When I got home from the Coop shows Greg and I went right to rehearsals. Ritchie and most of the band lived on Long Island, so this made going to rehearsal more like a day job. There would be a couple of weeks rehearsing before we went to Europe and then Japan. It was strange doing keyboards only, all the programming was done and without guitars to tune and maintain there wasn't a whole lot to do, but we did get all the equipment ready for the tour.

When the band was done rehearsing we flew to Copenhagen, Denmark for our production rehearsals. We would be working at an arena called KB Hallen, right in Copenhagen. When I heard about the initial arrangements I was not happy. We would be working at the arena and instead of hotels, the tour bus was parked outside and we lived there. I had never had to do anything like this before, and I thought that it was not professional at all. I have to admit, I actually liked this arrangement. There were showers at the arena, television on the bus, and we were downtown if you wanted to go out. There was no shuttling back and forth to the hotel, dragging your crap through the lobby. On tour I have always liked doing a lot of shows in a row with no hotel; it's just easier living on the bus. So this plan that I hated turned out to work well for me. We did four days of full rehearsals at the arena, but we would be coming back to do a show here, our first show was actually in Helsinki, Finland in a couple of days.

The shows with Rainbow were a collection of classic Deep Purple and Rainbow songs, plus the new cd, the show rocked. Since I wasn't tuning guitars all night I got to enjoy the music more than I normally would. The keyboard player Paul did need things during the show, but not too much. I mostly listened to the music and waited for something to break so I could fix it. On stage there was also a show within the show that I would watch every night. Ritchie's guitar tech Scott would be rocking out behind the amp line during the whole show. He was hired by Ritchie because he was a friend, he didn't have any experience at all with guitars, and he didn't seem to have any aptitude to learn. His first few gigs he just handed Ritchie an out of tune guitar, and didn't even have any spares out of the case. Ritchie had been at this so long he could make do with anything, and I think he liked the challenge.

At the end of each show Ritchie would lay his guitar on the edge of the stage and walk away. Normally, a guitar tech would retrieve it, retune it, and have it ready for the encore. Scott would be so busy giving the band a high five as they walked off, when they came on for the encore it was always a scramble to find the guitar. There was even one gig when the band went on stage and Ritchie's guitar couldn't be found. The rest of the band started jamming, and the singer Doogie started singing "Someone's stolen Ritchie's guitar". After a few minutes of this, a kid appeared at the back of the gig, guitar held high over his head, and proudly marched toward the stage. When he got close he handed the guitar back to Ritchie and the band played on. It turned out that he had stolen the guitar and had made it to the exit door when he heard the band singing about the guitar being stolen, which made him feel bad, so he came back to return it. All the while Scott never noticed that the guitar was gone. One of the other crew guys had been with Ritchie for over twenty years and he would tell us stories like this all the time. None of this was new in the Rainbow camp.

The singer in the band was a guy named Doogie White, who turned out to be a great singer and a cool guy. It wasn't long before Doogie, Greg and I became fixtures at various pubs along the tour. It was always a laugh hanging out with them, they would usually end up playing and singing at whatever pub we were in, and that was always my cue to start rustling up some free drinks for the effort. Ritchie and most of the band were into the old traditional British pub songs, which I also love.

The tour rolled through Europe and Scandinavia, we played all sorts of gigs on this one. Depending on the country we might be at a small theater or we could be at the local arena. Some of the gigs like Volkshaus in Zurich, Switzerland were near impossible to fit the show into. It took all day just to load in, forget sound check. The European leg of the tour ended with two shows at Hammersmith Apollo in London. After the shows we had a couple of days off while our gear was freighted over to Japan for the next leg. I have always loved London, so I made the most of this vacation.

For the Japan leg of the tour we would of course be working with Udo Artists, which was great. We would be doing shows all over the country, some cities I had never been to before. In Japan they respect guitar players and over there Ritchie was a music icon. He could play there anytime he wanted, without a record out, and sell out. We started the tour with two shows in Tokyo at the Yoyogi Olympic Pool, which was about nine thousand capacity. After that we played in Kyoto, Osaka, Nagoya, back to Osaka, then Kitakyishu, Yokahama, and then back to Tokyo for one more show.

Everything went great and the Udo people were perfect, as usual. The only surprise here was that this was my first time in Japan without seeing my old friend George Silk. He had moved his shop and I couldn't find him, although we were really busy this trip. After the last Tokyo show it was time to head home again. I hadn't seen my wife in almost three months by now and since these were the days before everyone had a cell phone we had limited our phone calls to one quick call a week. We would primarily stay in touch via fax machine. Not the best, but there weren't a lot of options back then.

KISS Reunion

Early in 1996, I was made aware of the upcoming KISS reunion tour. I was also told that even though Peter Criss had a drum tech, there would be a job for me; I just didn't know what I would be doing. Initially I was told that Gene wanted me back as his bass tech, but one of the others crew guys from L.A. managed to get that gig while I was out of town. I don't know how, it doesn't matter.

Arrangements had been made for me to be part of the crew setting up the press conference that was to take place on the USS Intrepid in April. A lot of the displays from the convention tour were going to be set up all over the ship, so a few of us were recruited.

The press conference was a big deal, a precursor to one of the biggest tours of the year. While we were working on setting this up, I got a chance to talk to Tim, our production manager about my role on the upcoming tour. I wanted to make sure I had a definite spot, so that if there was any doubt I could find another tour. He told Todd Confessore and me that we would be part of a special effects crew, taking care of all the extras needed for the effects the tour would have. This was going to involve special fog effects, placement for fire effects, hydraulic amp walls. It all sounded cool and I was glad that I was going to be a part of it.

The press conference went off without a hitch and afterwards it was obvious that we would be gearing up for something big. I went home figuring it would be about six weeks until I would be heading out to rehearsals, which was about right. I flew out to California the beginning of June to get started.

When Todd and I got out the airplane hangar where we would be working, we met the carpentry crew that we would be working with. Since we had last talked about the gig, the special effects and carpentry crews had been rolled into one crew. We would also be building the stage, the barricade, the stage set, and doing a lot of custom fabrication. I was a little unsure of all this, my primary background had always been backline, but Todd and I dug in and got started, we were determined that this was going to work.

The crew would usually leave the hotel at seven a.m. and get right to work. We set up staging and set pieces as they came in and started to figure out what needed to be fabricated. The band would usually come by in the late afternoon to check our progress. After a few days they started to run through songs on the stage to get the feel of everything.

A typical day would start at seven in the morning and by the time we got out of there and got to bed it was usually two a.m. The days were long and the work was hard, and after a couple of weeks I had my doubts about whether or not I had the skills to do this tour. In the first month of rehearsals I lost thirty pounds. I'm no wimp, but when I say the work was hard, it was.

After the first gig, the Weenie Roast in California, we packed up and went to Detroit to get ready for the first stop on the tour, Tiger Stadium. By now I knew in my heart that as loyal to KISS as I was, I was not going to last on this tour. I spoke to the powers that be and it was a mutual parting on the best of terms. It would be better for me to do another tour, and it would be better for KISS to have a more experienced carpenter.

The door was opened for my return to the fold a few years later when Eric Singer rejoined the band. He called and asked me to come back as his drum tech, and as much as I wanted to, I had already made the decision to stay home and not tour anymore. So it was with much regret that I said no thank you.

Back with Alice Cooper

After leaving the KISS tour I immediately started making phone calls to everyone I knew in the business, to let them know I was looking for work. It was only a matter of a couple of days before one of the management from the Alice Cooper camp called and asked if I wanted to come out the next day and do the rest of the summer tour. Perfect I thought, at least I'll be working for the next three months. That would give me time to find something else to fill out the rest of the year.

One of the guitar techs on the Cooper tour had a family emergency and had to leave the tour right away. Hiring me worked out great for all parties involved. I knew the crew, the songs and how everything worked. They could just fly me in on a gig day, give me a set list with my cues on it, and I could do the show that night, which I did. I was working stage right for Ryan Roxie, the guitar player, and Todd Jensen, the bass player. I hadn't met either of them before so when they saw there was a new tech I think they were both a little apprehensive, and I can't blame them. But the show went fine and afterwards they both relaxed a little bit. We all ended up becoming friends and having a good time that summer.

The shows were always fun and it was good to be on a tour that I was better equipped to do, where I could feel confidant in my job. The crew guys had started a new tradition on this tour, camping on days off. On the days when there was going to be a long drive and we wouldn't get to the hotel until late anyway, we would get a buy out from production, basically they would give us each fifty dollars for saving them a hotel room. We would then pool all this extra money and buy food and beer with it. Plans would then be made to go to a campsite and spend the day instead of driving. We would eat, drink, barbeque and hang out all day. There was usually a pool or the ocean to go swimming. We would hang out and party until we were exhausted, then shower and get on the bus. The driver had been sleeping all day so we would all pass out while he drove, and we wouldn't wake up until we got to the gig the next morning.

The tour continued like this all summer, doing shows, camping, and just generally having a great time. I had heard the KISS tour was doing record business, but I still felt that I had made the right decision. By the end of the tour though I still hadn't found work to finish out the year and I was getting nervous. I kept putting feelers out, but I also prepared for a long slow fall in case there was no work. When the Cooper tour was over I was a little bummed, it had been a great time. But there was starting to be talk of working more often, so there was the prospect of another Cooper tour next year. Either way, I was heading home and hoping the phone was going to ring soon.

Tiny Music 96-97

And ring it did, the phone I mean. I had only been home a week, but it was a long week searching for work. One day I picked up the phone and heard "Hey Kenny, it's Dean, how's it going?" I replied, Dean who? I really had no idea. "Dean from STP" was his reply. Holy crap I thought, what does he want? I told him it was good to hear from him, it had been a long time. He told me that STP were rehearsing out in L.A., and wanted to know when I could fly out to rehearse and start the tour. I hadn't heard from any of the STP guys in two years, so I was surprised at this call. I worked out the details and the next thing I knew I was on a plane to California and I was back to work. That's how it is; you never know what's around the next corner or down the alley, see my dark alley analogy as mentioned earlier in the Meat Loaf section.

A couple of days later I was back in Los Angeles rehearsing with the band. The day I flew in I went straight to rehearsal where I was greeted like a returning family member. The guys stopped playing and everyone came over and hugged me. I had flown out with apprehensions but now I was starting to think this might work out better than I thought. I ran the set with the guys that day and started prepping gear for the tour. There is a certain routine you fall into once you get started. I was living near all the old book stores and memorabilia shops, I love old Hollywood. I would always head out early and check out the used book stores along the way. Once the band got comfortable with the set, we moved venues and started production rehearsals. This tour the band had been booked into larger buildings; their records had always been strong performers. STP was even booked into Madison Square Garden, and if I'm not mistaken, they sold it out.

The band was tight and they sounded great, the machine was definitely firing on all cylinders. The new show involved projection, which they seemed to like incorporating into their show, and it looked great. The tour started up, and while there were a few production bumps along the way, things worked out and the machine was purring along. The gig at Madison Square was one of those special nights you always hear about. The stars lined up and everything was perfect. Steven and Joe from Aerosmith came down and played a couple of songs, it was amazing.

On Thanksgiving we were in New York City to do the David Letterman Show. I've always liked Dave, and he has always gone out of his way for anyone on his show. Since we were there for the holiday, provisions had been made for all of us to have a proper Thanksgiving dinner with all the trimmings. We all took our food out to the bus and had our own holiday. Earlier in the day I went out to find a pay phone so I could call my wife and wish her a Happy Thanksgiving. I found a phone in front of the building we were working in, and made the call. While I was talking to her I heard something loud coming my way, we were having trouble hearing each other. I turned to see what it was, and I saw the Macy's Thanksgiving Day Parade heading right for me. I had a front row seat and didn't even know it.

The tour was set up so that we would work right up until Christmas and then go home, after that there was a Miller show in Vancouver on December 29, a show in Anchorage, Alaska on New Year's Eve and then fly to Hawaii for two shows and a week vacation with the wives. After that we would be heading out for another leg in the spring.

I flew up to Vancouver two days after Christmas for the first show. It was a Miller blind date where contest winners were flown to an unknown destination to see a surprise band. We would be loading into a club called Richard's on Richards, the venue for the event. The day of the show it had started to snow a bit, but we didn't really think anything of it. The band were going to meet up in Los Angeles at the airport and fly up together later in the day.

We got all our band and sound equipment in the club and filled the place with our cases alone. The first goal was to empty the road cases so we would have some room to work. While we were doing this the bands sound guy Jimmy Huth came over to us and told us to slow down. He had been on the phone with the band and I guess something was going on. Later on he told us to stop working and just hang out. This kind of thing is never good, we had no idea what was happening. A little while later we were told to start packing it back up. The band had met at the airport in Los Angeles and an issue came up between them that caused them to cancel the gig. Not just the Vancouver gig, Alaska, Hawaii and the vacation were all cancelled.

We packed everything back into the truck and went to the hotel; it was snowing pretty hard now. I had the unpleasant task of telling my wife that Hawaii was cancelled and I would be coming home early. She was disappointed, but she understood. The next morning I tried to fly home, but the snowstorm in Vancouver had turned into a blizzard and there were no flights out, the city had started to shut down. It took me three days to get out of Vancouver and get home. I arrived in Florida on New Year's Eve just in time to celebrate with my wife and some friends.

As far as any of us on the crew knew, all future tour plans had been cancelled. What had started out so promising had fallen apart as I looked on with amazement. STP was a great band and the new record was a big hit. These guys should have been on the road for two years, we barely made it three months. Early in January I got word that the band was in the process of putting together tour dates for the spring, and they wanted to keep the crew they had, so we were all staying on payroll until the next leg of the tour started. It was a relief that the checks were still coming in but any feeling of security was gone by now. There was always the possibility that it could all end tomorrow.

I went back to Los Angeles to start rehearsing in March. There had been some changes in crew, most notably our drum tech Cole had decided to leave. My old friend Todd Confessore was able to get the gig, so there was an old familiar face in the STP camp. Rehearsals started out well and the band had seemed to come to terms with their issues. We were able to work not matter what else went on. The tour headed out again and it seemed like the old days, we were having fun. One new thing on this leg was the addition of a crew band to sound check. It was comprised of me playing bass, Richie the bass tech playing guitar, Todd on drums and Scott from the sound crew singing. At first the rest of the crew named us "The Hated" because we were so bad, but after a while we got to be not so bad. One night while drinking, my old friend Putter T was telling me that we were about as dangerous as a bunch of monkeys with guns. That was it; it stuck; now we were "Monkeys with Guns".

I didn't know it at the time, but one of the guys in the band had started asking the sound guy to record our sound check so that he could listen. After a while I guess he decided we weren't too bad, one afternoon not long before show I was told, "You guys are going on tonight after Cheap Trick". So that was it, on May 7, 1997 Monkeys with Guns made their debut at Oak Mountain Amphitheatre in front of about eleven thousand people. I was nervous at first but we started having fun with it. Just before the first song ended the band came walking out ready to play and the crowd went wild for them. I have a video of this; I need to post it on the web one day.

The tour continued to go well and before I knew it we were at the last gig in San Diego. There is an old road tradition of pulling stunts on the band the last gig of the tour. This can be tricky as some people can be cool with this and others not. I don't think the guys in KISS would ever let this be done to them. It's a fine line. We had a few things in mind for STP and they knew it, they just didn't know when or what. Nothing was done for the first part of the show and the band guys kept looking over their shoulders waiting.

In the middle of the show there was an acoustic section where a platform decorated with pillows and rugs would come down from the ceiling and the guys would play from up there. Normally I would walk out on stage to hand Dean his first acoustic guitar, a cherished instrument he had had for years. Earlier in the day I had gotten a cheap look alike for this gig. As I walked the guitar out to him I pretended to trip and fall on it, flattening it completely. I looked up and the four band guys were all staring at me with dropped jaws. They thought it was real, the guitar destroyed and me possibly hurt. I was later told that you could hear the impact all the way out at the sound board. After a minute I handed Dean the real guitar and the guys spent the acoustic set laughing and shaking their heads.

The guys knew it was on now, and it was. There were a lot of antics that night not the least of which was a full on marching band that paraded across the stage during the show. The whole last gig turned out to be memorable, there were some stunts pulled that I never would have thought of. This crew had all gelled and worked together so well, it had become a family in a short amount of time. It had been a good tour and I was sorry to see it end. Things had been so much better than my previous gig with these guys.

Alice Cooper 1997

I've come to realize that a lot of these chapters begin the same way, "Tour number one ended, and before I knew it, I was rehearsing for tour number two". It's funny looking back on it today, but there were a lot of patterns in my career, and it's hard to write about them without seeming redundant. Keeping that in mind I have to say that when the STP tour ended it wasn't long before I was out rehearsing for the next Alice Cooper tour.

The Rock 'N Roll Carnival tour was booked for Europe, The States and Australia with the rehearsals in London and the first show in Hamburg, Germany. There were a lot of the usual suspects on this tour, Ralph, Batty, Putter, J Mann and Tater. The rehearsals were right near the antiques district in London so whenever there was a break I would usually sneak out and see what I could find. A lot of times at the rehearsal place I could be found in the office boxing up whatever I had found, or running to the post office to ship the items home. I even bought a student desk that I had arranged to pick up when we came back to London. I boxed it up and took it on the plane with me. Back in the day airplane restrictions were nothing like they are now. During the tour I found some cool antiques in Germany that I was able to put in road cases for the trip home.

This was the Rock 'N Roll Carnival tour and the stage looked like a dilapidated old circus, which had a cool look to it. Alice would make his entrance from a giant toy box stage right. The overall look and theme to the show worked well wherever we went. We covered a lot of ground on this tour, starting in London. From there it was Germany, Holland, back to Germany, the Czech Republic, Poland, Austria, Hungary, Belgium, France, England, Scotland, back to England, Spain, Italy, Switzerland, back to Germany, and then home. That was a lot of travel for a little over a month. We did a lot of shows and for a change there wasn't a lot of time to go sight seeing, although I did make time to go pick up my student desk in London. We also had a little time to go to the Vatican when we were in Italy.

The U.S. leg of the tour was just as busy. We started in Los Angeles with a few rehearsals before starting up again. The tour started in Colorado with a gig the next day in Illinois. We had to hurry out of the gig to make a charter flight that got us to Illinois at three a.m. and then we had to go straight to the gig. From there we picked up the buses and it got a bit easier. We worked our way through St. Paul, Detroit, Cincinnati, Milwaukee, you get the idea. These tour descriptions can get to be like a geography lesson.

The gig in Cincinnati was outdoors and there started to be bad rain and lightning. The promoter was afraid of losing the show and he let Putter know that it was important that everyone play. There was never any question that Alice would go on; I have still never seen him miss a show. Some of our support acts were a bit squeamish about performing with lightning striking so close, it had actually hit a street light not far from the gig, we had seen it from the stage. All in all the crew were able to convince the other three bands to go on and do a couple of songs. The promoter was happy and he took care of us after the show.

The tour continued much the same across the U.S., we wound our way east and then headed back west through Texas, Arizona, Nevada and back to California. We had a little time off in L.A. because we were heading to Australia next and the gear needed to be shipped. After a couple of days hanging out we got on a plane and took that long wonderful flight back to Australia. I still always think of my first production manager Omar when I go to Australia, he's the one that described to me how far it was in drinking terms.

The Australian leg of the tour was being handled by Lennard Promotions, and they turned out to be great. I hadn't worked with them before but they ended up helping me when I needed it. We got to Perth on September third and the first gig was on the fifth. We all went to the gig to go through our gear to make sure all was well, and then of course we went out. Some of the guys hadn't been to Australia before, so there was a little sight seeing and shopping. Later that night after a few drinks Tater, J Mann and I were walking to another pub when suddenly I had to go, and there was no place to relieve myself. I did my best but by the time we got somewhere I could go my walk was so contorted from holding it, I looked like I had something wrong with me. This walk was later named the "Dance of Dr. Zaius" for reasons I still don't know.

Early the next morning my wife called me at the hotel. There was a family emergency back home in Florida and I needed to get home ASAP. I told her to give me some time to see what I could do. I called Putter to let him know what was up and he called the promoter, Lennard Promotions to see what they could do. In less than an hour arrangements had been made, right after the gig that night there would be a car to take me to the airport, and there were stand-by arrangements all the way home. That afternoon I told the band guys I had to go. We got through the show; I put my guitars away, walked off stage and into a car and never looked back. We drove to the airport where I waited stand-by for about five hours for the flight to Sydney, from Sydney to Los Angeles, Los Angeles to Orlando and then into a waiting car to drive me home. All told between travel and stand-by time it took me fifty hours to get home, which didn't matter, I made it in time.

A lot of people worked hard to get me home when I needed it. The Cooper crew and management team were there for me, the promoter, Lennard Promotions, Coop and the band guys were all supportive. They had to deal with whatever tech that could be contacted in each city, and from what I heard, it wasn't pretty. Well anyway, thank you all, again. This was not the best way to end a tour, but I did get to see who was there for me.

Talk Show

Three of the guys from STP, Dean, Robert and Eric had formed a new band with singer Dave Coutts, called Talk Show. I thought the record they did was cool, so when they decided to tour behind it I thought it would be a good gig to take. This was going to be a lot different than the STP days; we were going out opening for The Foo Fighters in small theaters, clubs and colleges, and the second leg we would be opening for Aerosmith in arenas. We all traveled on one bus and had a small truck with our gear traveling with us.

It was fun starting over like this, the band was new and every day was a new adventure. The gigs with The Foo Fighters were cool, but a lot of them were tough load ins, and as the support band usually we didn't get to sound check. By the time the Foos finished their check, the doors to the building usually opened and we had to just get our gear up there and do the best we could. That was one thing about STP, they always made sure that the other bands were taken care of and had time to check.

We traveled around the U.S. and Canada late in '97, doing shows like this, getting to clubs and hoping there was enough room for our gear. I have to say, the band guys never complained. Everyone made do with whatever we had, and we always got through the gig. There was one club where our gear had to be handed out from over the front of the stage, through the audience and out a side door. In fact, a lot of these gigs were like this, but I think that's where all our camaraderie came in. It really was the band and crew against the world, and I think we all got to be better friends because of it.

The next leg of the tour we were opening for Aerosmith, so this looked to be a bit better than the last leg. We were still the opening band, but we could get our gear into the arena and be ready to take the stage when Aerosmith was done. This came in handy as Aerosmith usually checked right up until doors also; we were still getting everything up there as quickly as possible and checking as fast as we could. One perk of this tour was getting to watch Aerosmith every night. I have always been a big fan, as were most of the guys. Another perk was that Aerosmith didn't do a lot of shows in a week. This gave us time for side trips and a lot of adventures. One day the guys decided to go to Carlsbad Caverns, another time I mentioned Roswell, New Mexico and the next thing I knew we were heading there. Later in the tour we went to Taos, New Mexico to go skiing for three days. This gig was more vacation than anything.

As the tour progressed it became apparent that the band didn't feel that Dave was working out. STP had one of the best front men in the business, so Dave did have some big shoes to fill. I think initially the plan was for Talk Show to tour and do another record and keep working it, but somewhere along the way the plan changed. I think that the guys realized what they had with STP, and my personal feeling was that they would be back, soon.

I was glad I had done this tour, the guys and I had finally become good friends. I continued to talk to Dean every now and then after the tour, something we had never done before. I figured I would be a lifer with STP in some capacity when they returned, so for now I would stay home and be a regular guy. I was surprised when I got a call from the bands manager

Steve about a year and a half later. He had called to apologize, the band were about to release their next record, Number Four, and they had forgotten to thank me. He assured me that this would be corrected in subsequent pressings, and it seemed to be a bigger deal to him than it was to me. I asked him if he could send me a copy and he said he would. I told him not to sweat it; I was cool with the omission of my name.

When he sent me a cd, he sent me a burned copy, not a retail one with liner notes and a cover. I thought that was odd, but I listened to what he sent me and I loved the disc. A week later the cd came out, so I went to the store and bought one just to check it out. That's where I saw what he was making such a big deal about. I wasn't thanked on the disc, but there was a long thank you to the crew that had stood by them or something like that. They named four guys, two I had worked with and two I didn't know. They had hired a new crew and thanked them for being there. There was even a picture of the crew in the liner notes. I'll never understand this kind of thing. I shouldn't have gotten bummed out about it, but I did. I called the guys to ask what was up, but no one returned my calls. I should have known better than to let it be personal.

A funny after story, six months later I got home from a vacation in Key West and I had two phone messages from the bands sound guy, he sounded panicked and was wanting to know where I was and when I could be there for rehearsal and the tour. I guess he hadn't called and the band was looking for me. I had already agreed to do the next Alice Cooper tour by now, so I declined the offer. I did save the phone messages; maybe I'll post them on the web.

Home

After the Talk Show tour I made the decision to leave the touring business for good. I had been married a few years now and my wife and I had moved to Florida to start building our life together, so I thought it was time. This was not an easy decision for me to make, but I knew it was the right one. I had secured steady employment in the entertainment industry here in Florida, so that was one less worry.

During this time I was fortunate in that Alice had started doing New Year's Eve shows, playing a couple of shows before and then a gig on New Year's Eve. These mini tours were great for me, I still had a couple of shows to do and a little travel to look forward to. I don't know if Coop still does this, but I would love to do them again.

In 1997 we played the Star Plaza Theatre in Indiana on December 29. Among the crew were my old friends Ralph, J Mann, and Kevin "Tater" McCarthy. It was good to see everyone again and do some shows. On December 30 we played The Orbit Room in Grand Rapids, Michigan and on New Year's we played the State Theatre in Detroit, Michigan. These shows were a lot of fun, and I started to look forward to them every year.

In 1998 I went out to do the New Year's run again, and this year among the crew were Ralph, Tater and my old friend Charlie Milton. There were a lot of other familiar faces on the tour, it was always good to see Alice and the band, the rest of the crew, Toby, Brian; I could go on and on. You get the idea. This time out we played a casino in Mississippi and two shows in Florida. The entire trip was a lot of fun and as always, I hoped they would do this again next year.

New Year's 1999 was a big one for everyone, the new millennium and all that. Alice was going to do just one show this year, at his restaurant in Phoenix. We would rehearse for a couple of days and then do the show for the event at Cooperstown. The difference this year was that the Cooper organization flew all our wives out, so the gig was like a private party for all of us. My wife Monica ended up having a great time and she got to hang out with people I had worked with for years. I didn't know it then, but the seeds had been sown that week for my return to the road. Alice had a tour in the works that would be more theatrical with a larger production, and rehearsals would be starting in a couple of months.

I think that after my wife came out for the gig and saw me doing what I do again, she realized that was who I was. In a couple of months when the offer came for me to do the next tour, she pushed me a little bit, knowing that I should do it. I'm glad she did.

Brutal Planet

Rehearsals for the Brutal Planet tour were in Phoenix, at a local theater. I was unable to commit a lot of time to rehearsing; I missed most of the band rehearsals and came out for production rehearsal with the full stage set. The new record was heavy and the stage looked like an industrial wasteland. There were some really cool set pieces that reminded me of the first Mad Max movie. I was working for Ryan Roxie again, and Teddy Zig Zag who played keyboards.

I know that throughout this book I have always said I was excited to do a tour for some reason or another. What can I say, I loved my work. This tour had a new element for me, we were going to Russia. I felt like Rocky in Rocky IV. We were also going to a few other countries I had never visited, Estonia, Lithuania, and Bulgaria. There were a lot of other stops on this tour as well, but it was nice to cover some new ground and see some new countries. We were also shooting the British show "Top of the Pops" at the BBC. The pyro tech that did our flame effects had worked on the BBC show "Red Dwarf" which was a favorite among the Cooper crew. We cornered that guy and peppered him with a ton of questions.

The first show on the tour was a festival in Sweden which was a little difficult. The show was being put together for the first time since rehearsals, and we were doing it on the fly. It came together but that was a long day. We were heading to Russia after the gig and as we were driving along we were passed by a guy on a motorcycle with a large satchel. A few of the guys were kidding saying wouldn't it be funny if that was the guy with our Russian visas, sort of like an old spy movie. A minute later the bus pulled over and our tour manager got out and met the guy on a motorcycle under an overpass up ahead. An exchange was made and the tour manager was back on the bus handing out passports, which had all the Russian paperwork done. Nobody asked about the guy on the motorcycle, we didn't really want to know.

Russia really is quite beautiful when you look at it. St. Petersburg was a bit dreary but Moscow was a lot like Manhattan, I was surprised. Having grown up during the tail end of the cold war we were always told that Russian women were all weightlifters with moustaches, well I can tell you far from it. There were a lot of beautiful women on the streets of Moscow. I guess propaganda goes both ways and we were guilty of it too.

The Brutal Planet tour hammered through Europe as all Cooper tours do, we worked a lot and played anywhere. When we got to Bulgaria the promoters were very thankful, it seems a lot of bands book shows there, but most cancel when they start dealing with the logistical nightmare of getting there. We were loading into an old army stadium outside of town, and they really weren't set up for a show. There were no amenities; there was no way to get food as there was nothing nearby. The caterers had put out what passed for deli trays but between the heat and the swarms of flies, it really wasn't worth chancing. We had every monitor board that was in Bulgaria, all three of them, tied together to get enough channels to do a show. It was hot as hell out and there was no place to go to get away from the heat. The electrical power that was supplied was another nightmare, the ground was for crap and most of our gear was buzzing and humming. We were working all day just to pull this off, not sure if we could. At one point our monitor guy Tater fell off the stage and injured himself. As we were hustling to get things ready we got the call from security, either we let the audience in, as they were getting crazy, or security was going to quit, which was not an option. Gigs like this could be a disaster without local security. The call was made, let the audience in. We continued to try and pull this off until we got the word, ready or not we're going on. Coop and the band came up, and went on with what we had. Monitors were buzzing and cutting out, wireless packs were failing and when you thought you had seen it all, it started raining. With all the equipment problems and the rain blowing in onto the stage you can almost guess how the night went, it rocked. I've said it before, it's these gigs where you're all up against it that you see what everyone is made of and nail it. Coop nailed it. No songs were cut; the show wasn't shortened in any way, rain or not. Countries like Bulgaria are so starved for entertainment that when they do get a show, it's a huge deal. They were out there in the rain with us, rocking hard.

After load out we were shuttled to the nearest shower two at a time. J Mann and I were driven through the woods for about forty five minutes and taken to some small athletic club to shower. It was about two in the morning and we were left there with the locals to fend for ourselves for an hour and a half, with no guarantee that anyone was coming back to get us. We both looked at each other and laughed, we were in Bulgaria but we didn't know where, we had no money on us, if our ride didn't come back we were screwed. Of course our ride did come back and I did

make it home safely. I had to; we still had the U.S.
leg of the tour to do.

Bulgaria from my hotel room

Russia 2000

Russia 2000

Russia 2000

One of our truck drivers on this leg traveled with his dog, Pedro.

Brutal in the U.S.

We started the U.S. leg of the tour early in September 2000. From our first gig in New York we headed west stopping in Cleveland, Detroit, the usual geography lesson. After some of the gigs and drives on the last leg, it was good to get home. By now there had started to be a little friction amongst the crew, which can be normal. Sometimes these things work themselves out, sometimes not, just another day on the Brutal Planet. I did forget to mention in the last chapter that we played German Bike Week with the German division of Hell's Angels as our stagehands. There was a big Viking style ceremony on stage and by then all the stage hands were drunk. We ended up loading our own trucks while they broke beer bottles. After that anything else seems tame. Except the girl in Maine we met who had a picture of her dead boyfriends tombstone tattooed on her back. Like I said, it was good to be back in the U.S. I love the rest of the world, but I really like coming home. This leg of the tour we had a great support band, Dope, with us. The shows were all good as usual. By now there really isn't anything new to add. Since the Brutal tour I've done one offs here and there, (That's a single gig to those that don't know). I hear from the old road brothers now and then, a couple of weeks ago Blake was in town and we hooked up.

If you've noticed that there isn't any dirt in here, it's intentional. There is good and bad in anything, but I loved my days on the road. It isn't worth even thinking about what some loser might have done years ago. All that matters is the good stuff, the shows, the people, the Bigga Gigs.

Today

As I sit here today, May 5, 2009, I have just finished writing this book. I started in May of 2008, twelve months ago, and I thought I could get this project done in a few weeks. In that time I've had a few things come up where I didn't lay a hand on this book for a month or more. There were a few times I almost said screw it and threw it away. I have tried to condense over twenty years into a couple of hundred pages and in doing so I have learned a lot. I think that anyone that goes out on even one tour could write a book like this. One tour is enough to fill it and then some.

I've been giving thought to expanding this idea; maybe do a book about all my tours with Alice Cooper, or one about my years on the road with KISS. This would give me the chance to give more of a day to day perspective, as though the reader was there. Can "We Are the Road Crew: The KISS Years" be far behind? While working on this I have revisited a part of my life I hadn't thought about in a long time. As I have been writing I have been remembering more and more. There are definitely a few more books here. Time will tell.

Ken Barr
May 2009

37269106R00131

Made in the USA
Lexington, KY
25 November 2014